Middle

—— · Tales of · ——

MYSTERY
& MURDER

Other areas covered in this series include:

Berkshire	Lancashire
Buckinghamshire	Leicestershire & Rutland
Cheshire	Lincolnshire
Cornwall	Northamptonshire
Derbyshire	Nottinghamshire
Devon	Somerset
East Anglia	Staffordshire
Essex	Surrey
Hampshire	Sussex
Hertfordshire	Warwickshire
Kent	Wiltshire

Middlesex
Tales of

MYSTERY
& MURDER

Mike Hall

COUNTRYSIDE BOOKS
NEWBURY BERKSHIRE

First published 2005
© Mike Hall 2005

COUNTRYSIDE BOOKS
3 Catherine Road
Newbury, Berkshire

To view our complete range of books,
please visit us at
www.countrysidebooks.co.uk

ISBN 1 85306 919 1
EAN 978 1 85306 919 2

Designed by Peter Davies, Nautilus Design
Produced through MRM Associates Ltd., Reading
Typeset by Techniset Typesetters, Newton-le-Willows
Printed by J. W. Arrowsmith Ltd., Bristol

Contents

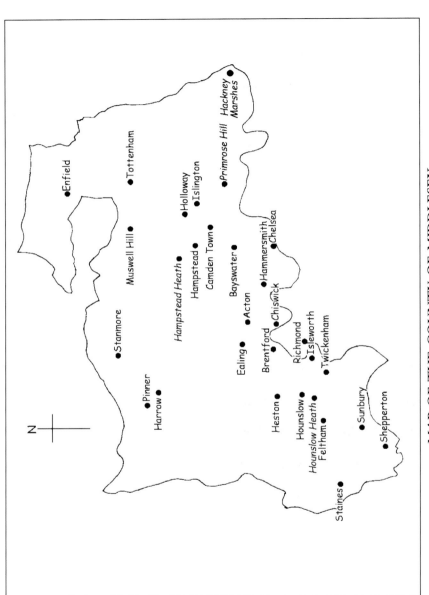

MAP OF THE COUNTY OF MIDDLESEX

INTRODUCTION

———————— ❁ ————————

Middlesex, as a county, may seem hardly synonymous with mystery. It lacks the romance that is associated with places like Cornwall or Somerset. There are no magical Middlesex legends, no whimsical hippie trail wending its way from Staines to Edmonton via Hendon and Muswell Hill. R. D. Blackmore's *Lorna Doone* spawned a whole tourist industry around Exmoor, but his *Kit and Kitty*, set around Hanworth and Sunbury has singularly failed to do the same for Middlesex, despite the fact that Blackmore was a Teddington man for much of his working life.

This makes it difficult for an author charged with the task of writing a book called *Middlesex Tales of Mystery & Murder*. There are plenty of murders – and I shall come to them shortly – but the county hides its mysterious past well. Nevertheless, it does exist and there are strange tales of ancient monuments such as Caesar's Camp and Grim's Dyke. Queen Boadicea's grave may lie within the former boundary of the county and parts of West Middlesex are covered by the enigmatic Kingston Zodiac, described by Mary Caine in a book published as recently as 2001.

Stories of ghosts are easier to find. Many were described in my previous book, *Haunted Places of Middlesex*, but there are more here, from strange encounters in the Kings Road to the erotic visions of two young women that troubled a retired accountant at his bungalow in Shepperton in 2004.

Murder has sadly been a constant feature of Middlesex life as long as there have been people living here. Sometimes it was the accidental result of over-zealous law enforcement as in the case of John White, the soldier who died after a flogging at Hounslow Barracks in 1846 – but often it is simply the result of the sordid realities of crime or lust. Out of respect for the victims' families, I have not included very recent murders but human nature has not changed over the years and many of the killings that I describe have a contemporary feel to them.

As readers of local papers will know, there are still some strange stories out there!

Mike Hall

WALTER SICKERT
AND THE CAMDEN
TOWN MURDER

❁

The murder at 29 St Paul's Road (now Agar Grove), Camden Town, on 12th September 1907 had everything the sensation-loving Edwardian public craved in the way of titillation: a woman killed in her sleep; the discovery, by her lover, of her naked body with its throat cut; his grief; the long search for the murderer who had slipped away into the night; the eventual arrest of the prime suspect; and a charismatic defence counsel who brought about a sensational acquittal. Added to this, more recently, is the claim that a renowned and celebrated artist of the period was, in fact, the murderer and, indeed, was none other than Jack the Ripper himself!

No 29 St Paul's Road was rented by Bertram Shaw, a chef on the railways, whose job meant that he was seldom at home overnight. This was very convenient for Emily (who was also known as Phyllis) Dimmock. She called herself Mrs Shaw but worked as a prostitute, picking up clients in local pubs and taking them back to the empty upstairs rooms. In the shabby backwater that was St Paul's Road, no questions were asked and she found the 'work' easier and more agreeable than the domestic service in East Finchley that had been her previous employment.

For three consecutive nights, her client had been a ship's cook making the most of his time ashore. Emily must have given satisfaction because he was keen to go with her again but she put him off, showing him a letter and a postcard, allegedly from two different people making appointments to meet her at different pubs that night. On the postcard the name of the Rising Sun was indicated by a pretty little sketch showing the sun peeping over the horizon. He might have thought it odd that these communications, the letter from 'Bert' and the postcard from 'Alice', were both in the same handwriting but, if he did, he was too polite – or perhaps too disappointed – to say so.

The next morning Bertram Shaw returned home to find Emily's body in the locked bedroom, unclothed and with her throat cut. He was clearly not the Bert who had written the letter (which was later found charred in the fireplace) and both he and the ship's cook were found to have unshakeable alibis for the time the crime must have been committed. Suspicion now centred on a young man seen in Emily's company in the Eagle pub several times in the past few weeks.

The postcard, with its distinctive drawing of the rising sun, was a vital clue. It was published in the newspapers and recognised by another prostitute, Ruby Young, as the work of one of her clients, a young graphic artist named Robert Wood. Wood was employed as an artist

29 St Paul's Road (now Agar Grove) where Phyllis Dimmock was murdered.

and engraver in a glassworks in Holborn. He had considerable talent and had attracted the support and encouragement of the great William Morris.

Over several months, Robert Wood's relationship with Ruby had moved on from being a purely business arrangement and, although he had recently discarded her, Ruby was still fond of him and decided not to inform the police despite the £100 reward on offer from the *News of the World*. However, she did tell a friend who then told someone else and soon Wood found himself under arrest.

The case against him seemed pretty strong. Wood knew Emily Dimmock and had frequently availed himself of her services. The prosecution brought forward several witnesses who identified Wood as being with her in the Eagle that night and he had been seen leaving number 29 St Paul's Road at dawn. There was no doubt that he must have been the last person to have seen her alive. As Martin Fido put it in *Murder Guide to London* (1986), 'one bloodstain on his clothing must surely have hanged him'.

But they had reckoned without Marshall Hall, 'the Great Defender'. At the time this well-known star of the Old Bailey needed a success to revive his fortunes after his political ambitions had been dashed by defeat in the election the year before. He recognised that if he could succeed in getting Wood off, it would make his reputation. He also knew that this was one of those strange cases in which the public's sympathies, manipulated by the newspapers, lay almost entirely with the accused rather than the victim.

Marshall Hall cleverly exploited Wood's mild-mannered demeanour and innocent good looks. Speaking in answer to Hall's skilful promptings, he made a very favourable impression on the jury. When the Judge referred to Wood's 'immoral life', by which he meant his use of Emily as a prostitute, Hall sprang to his defence and would not be silenced. 'I want to point out in the interests of justice,' he said dramatically, 'that there is not a particle of evidence that the prisoner ever had improper intercourse with Emily Dimmock.'

When the 'Not guilty' verdict was announced, there was applause in the courtroom and from the crowd waiting outside.

Had the great advocate's eloquence been in a just cause or had it brought about a miscarriage of justice?

In October 2002, a television documentary, *In Search of the Ripper*, came up with the startling accusation, made by the crime writer Patricia Cornwell, that Robert Wood was indeed innocent and that the real murderer was the artist Walter Sickert – and that Sickert had, in fact, also carried out the 'Jack the Ripper' killings some twenty years before. Cornwell had certainly done her homework, even to the extent of minutely examining one of Sickert's paintings in an attempt to extract his DNA.

Certainly Walter Sickert, a well known and respected artist, was a strange man, attracted to the seedier side of life. He had lived in Camden and painted a series of pictures called *The Camden Town Murders*. One of these shows a man – allegedly, Wood – sitting on the edge of a bed on which lies a naked woman, her head turned away and partially in shadow. Patricia Cornwell suggests that Sickert had used the dead Emily as a real-life model for this gruesome tableau. The basis for her claim was a contemporary report in the *Daily Telegraph* in which Sickert apparently claimed to have sketched the scene. From this she makes the link to the Jack the Ripper killings and accuses Sickert of being the perpetrator of these as well.

The whole affair was considered by John Barber in a lengthy analysis available on the internet at www.johnbarber.com/CTM/sickert.html. He points out that 'although Patricia Cornwell has been given much media attention and sold many millions of books, she is not the first to put Walter Sickert in the frame'.

John Barber concludes that it is unlikely that Sickert was ever there to commit the murder of Emily Dimmock. 'I cannot see that there is any evidence connecting Walter Sickert to this murder,' he writes. 'It appears that Patricia Cornwell was searching for more murders to link with the serial killings in Whitechapel and has tried to make the suspect fit the crime.'

Surely, if Sickert had been there, his presence would have been mentioned by Bertram Shaw – it wasn't. 'To the best of my research,' Barber writes, 'Sickert had no connection with Emily. Bert and Emily lived quite a distance from Sickert's circle of influence and his name is never mentioned in any of the family's recollections. Nor by any of the contemporary biographers of Marshall Hall, all of whom had access to the transcripts of the trial.' None of the descriptions of men seen in the vicinity at crucial times match Sickert. Sickert's one-time mistress, Florence Pash, also believed that he had no involvement at all with the Camden Town murder.

Nor is it likely that the Camden Town murderer and Jack the Ripper were one and the same person. Barber points out that there was a nineteen-year interval between the Ripper murders and this one. This is a long gap for a serial killer and no similar crimes in those intervening years have come to light. The nature of the crimes was different – there was no ritual mutilation of Emily's body as there was with most of the Ripper killings. There was evidence that the Camden killer had made an attempt to clean up afterwards which was not the case in Whitechapel.

Whatever the truth of the matter, Sickert's painting of the young woman lying dead on her bed is a particularly poignant one.

A WORK OF
THE DEVIL?

———————— ✿ ————————

Grim's Dyke is an ancient earthwork, composed of a deep ditch and bank, that snakes its way from Pinner towards Harrow Weald and which is still visible along much of its course to this day. Variously attributed to the 5th or 6th century AD – or, contrastingly, to pre-Roman times – it conjures up an air of brooding mystery, unexpected in the outer suburbs. Its name suggests that our Anglo-Saxon ancestors regarded it as the work of the Devil. Yet, in the 20th century, it somewhat improbably gave its name to a telephone exchange serving parts of Middlesex in the days before the introduction of all-figure numbers!

Michael Collins, in his 1953 book on Middlesex, described how it could be followed intermittently from Cuckoo Hill at Pinner Green, from Woodridings School on Pinner Hill Road north-east towards the main railway line, then from Oxhey Lane parallel to Wealdwood Road and across the golf course and into the grounds of the house which, like the golf course, bears its name.

Collins quoted research by historian H. Braun, published in 1936, using evidence of old place-names to show that the dyke extended eastwards, beyond Harrow Weald, but there is nothing much to be seen there now. Braun apparently believed that the earthwork was constructed as an aid to hunting, channelling the hunters' quarry to make their sport easier. Another theory has it as marking a tribal boundary or a military defence line.

However, Mr Collins was unconvinced. 'It can hardly have been a military defence work,' he wrote, 'for it is sited quite uselessly for that purpose.' He went on: 'It is difficult to accept that so large a work could have been undertaken merely for the purpose of delimiting part of a tribal boundary or in connection with hunting. It remains a rather mysterious feature of the Middlesex landscape.'

Patricia Clarke in her *History of Pinner*, published in 2004, writes that Grim's Dyke 'may have been one ditch from the start, or a series of ditches, or unassociated pieces.' She adds that 'it conforms to no contour of height or geology, nor to the boundary of Middlesex.' Judging from the fact that the spoil from such an excavation was usually dumped on the diggers' side of the ditch in order to heighten the bank, the dyke looks like a boundary for land on the north side – but for what purpose?

She suggests that it would have been 'unusual and difficult' to drive such an earthwork through woodland, possible evidence that the land on one or both sides must at the time already have been cleared for farming, only to revert to woodland later.

The name Grim's Dyke (or Ditch) probably dates back to the Saxons. Similar features in the Chilterns and in Wiltshire are also named after Grim (the ancient pagan god, Woden) and, in the absence of any other explanation at the time, attributed to the Devil himself. Grim's name lives on in modern English in the word 'gremlin'. Were there ever strange diabolical happenings related to the earthwork?

Below the Dyke, near Pinner, shafts were dug in the early 19th century for the mining of chalk. The miners carved out subterranean galleries up to 20 feet high in the chalk, which was interlaced with bands of flint. Names or initials have been found carved into the chalk or scratched into the soot created by the candles that were the only illumination. The workings were reached by narrow shafts from the surface. Using ropes or ladders, the workers had to descend these shafts – they were barely five feet wide – and the chalk had to be hoisted up out of them. The work was mainly seasonal, being done when the requirement for farm labour was low. By the 1880s chalk was more easily obtained from large quarries in the Chilterns and elsewhere, transported by railway, and the mines under Grim's Dyke were abandoned.

The name Grim's Dyke was given to the distinctive picturesque house built at Harrow Weald to the design of the architect

Grim's Dyke, near Pinner.

Norman Shaw in 1872. 'Tall brick chimney stacks not hidden away but prominent and part of the design. Local bricks, local tiles, local timber. No facade is the same. Gabled windows gaze through leaded lights down winding lawns ... And yonder gloomy pool contained on May 29th 1911 the dead body of W. S. Gilbert, Grim's Dyke's most famous owner.' Thus Sir John Betjeman paid homage to the memory of Savoy Opera librettist William Schwenk Gilbert in his classic television programme *Metroland*, first broadcast in 1973.

By 1890, when Gilbert purchased Grim's Dyke, the most productive years of his collaboration with Sir Arthur Sullivan were behind him. Only *Utopia Limited* and *The Grand Duke* were still to be written. Gilbert had fallen in love with the house and its 29 acres of grounds. With the private fortune he had amassed from his lyrics, he assembled a private menagerie and grew tropical plants in a large hothouse in the garden. He often said that if he could choose the place of his death it would be in the garden at Grim's Dyke. He got his wish – but in tragic and rather suspicious circumstances which prompted probing questions from the coroner at the subsequent inquest.

By 1911 Gilbert had become very much the English country gentleman. He was a magistrate and Deputy Lieutenant of Middlesex, taking his duties very seriously. He gave financial support to a fund to pay for patrols of the open area of Harrow Weald, then much-frequented by footpads and vagabonds. He arranged parties for the local children and he welcomed visitors to his home and to enjoy the garden.

Let Sir John take up the story once more: 'After a good luncheon,' he wrote, 'Gilbert went bathing with two girls, Ruby Preece and Winifred Emery. Ruby was out of her depth and, in rescuing her, Gilbert died of a heart attack, here – in this pond.'

The inquest was held in the billiard room at Grim's Dyke by Dr Gordon Hogg, the coroner for West Middlesex. The foreman of the jury was Mr A. Helsham-Jones, JP, a resident of Pinner and an old family friend. He seems to have had concerns about the propriety of 74-year-old Gilbert bathing with two young maiden ladies and was anxious to ensure that the details were kept out of the newspapers. 'Mr Helsham-Jones had a whispered consultation with the Coroner,' an article in the *Middlesex Quarterly* (1955) quoted from a contemporary account. 'Dr Hogg said very emphatically that he could not interfere with the Press at all and that the suppression of the names very often gave rise to much that was objectionable.'

Dr Hogg reported that when Miss Preece got into difficulties Gilbert swam very fast to her, telling her not to splash. 'It'll be all right,' he told her – but these were the last words he uttered. As he got to her, he placed her hand on his shoulder and then suddenly sank. The two women shouted out for assistance. The gardeners came with a boat and rowed out to Gilbert's body. When he was taken out of the water, attempts were made to revive him but to no avail.

Gilbert's own physician, Dr W. W. Shackleton of Bushey, told the inquest that the deceased had 'high tension and an intermittent pulse' and that he had warned him against swimming in the lake when it was too cold. He gave the cause of death as heart failure due to excessive exertion. Miss Preece gave evidence and her story confirmed what the jury had already been told. To speak of what had happened must have been quite an ordeal for her – did she, I wonder, feel in some way responsible for the old man's death?

Tactfully, Dr Hogg concluded: 'Undoubtedly he died in the effort to save this young lady in distress, which I think is a very honourable end to a distinguished career.' That is undoubtedly the truth of the matter. But is it the whole truth?

Gilbert's Pool at Grim's Dyke.

I visited Grim's Dyke in May 2005, 94 years almost to the day since Gilbert's tragic death. It turned out to be the hottest day in May since 1944 as I toiled up through the woods from Stanmore. Grim's Dyke is now a very grand hotel approached up a drive flanked by massive rhododendron bushes. The house looks magnificent, set amid immaculate lawns and formal gardens but it has to be said that Gilbert's Pool itself came as something of a disappointment. Following a sign on the far side of the house, I walked down a straight path through some woodland to discover a muddy depression, overgrown with marsh vegetation. Perhaps it was due to the dry weather that spring but, whatever the cause, there would have been no prospect of anyone drowning there – although they might have got stuck in the mud!

THE TRIDENT
DISASTER

Imagine the horror that must have been felt by drivers on the Staines by-pass on the afternoon of Sunday, 18th June 1972 as a BEA Trident dropped out of the sky in front of them and plunged into a field next to the road. One hundred and eighteen people died in what was Britain's worst air crash before Lockerbie. How could it happen? Why did a well-maintained aircraft with an excellent safety record and under the command of an experienced and skilled pilot come to such a tragic end?

Despite bad weather conditions (low cloud, rain and blustery winds), the take-off of flight BE 548 to Brussels was quite normal and gave no cause for concern. The plane was full to capacity because an airline strike on the Continent had caused many passengers to transfer to the BEA service. Two minutes into the flight the aircraft stalled and barely half a minute later hit the ground with the loss of life of everyone on board. It was later stated that if the plane had remained airborne for just a few more seconds it would have come down on the centre of Staines itself with horrific consequences.

The disaster was witnessed by two boys, who ran half a mile to summon assistance. Among the first to arrive was Frances Castledine, a trained nurse, along with a man from the St John Ambulance Brigade and a police constable from Feltham. There was nothing that they could do. Bodies were lying all around, with passengers hanging out of the plane's windows. Among the dead were three-year-old twin sisters. One victim was still alive but in terrible pain from injuries to his legs. They got him out onto the grass but he died almost immediately. Another passenger was taken from the scene alive but unconscious. He died in hospital three hours later. Those first on the scene commented afterwards on the eerie silence.

It was not quiet for long. As news spread crowds of sightseers gathered, some with children on their shoulders. An ice-cream van appeared, its owner untroubled by the nature of his unexpected business opportunity. There was even a religious fanatic carrying a biblical slogan on a placard. The rescue services were appalled at the antics of these ghouls and shouted at them to go away. If any of the passengers and crew had still been alive, their rescue would have been seriously hampered by the crowds of onlookers whose vehicles were now parked nose to tail alongside the road. Perhaps some of those involved are now ashamed of their actions.

Onlookers gathered around the scene of the crash. (Surrey Herald and News)

One alarming fact, soon discovered, was that this particular aircraft had been in a fatal accident before. In July 1968 a freightliner carrying horses had veered off the runway as it landed at Heathrow, smashing through the tailfin of the BEA Trident and slicing off the rear fuselage of another plane before hitting the front of the newly-built Terminal One. Six people aboard the freightliner were killed and 28 airport workers on the ground were injured. However, BEA engineers were able to repair the Trident and it was back in service after eight months. Clearly the 1968 accident had no bearing on the crash at Staines.

Investigators soon pinpointed the immediate cause – the premature retraction of the droops, the device hinged at the bottom of the leading edge of the wing which provides additional lift while the plane is taking off and climbing to its cruising speed. They should not have been retracted until the aircraft had climbed another 1,300 feet and was flying considerably faster.

This discovery only led to more questions. Why was such a basic error committed in the first place and then not immediately corrected by the flight crew, alerted by the plane's safety equipment? There would have been plenty of visual and audible warnings that something was wrong – and there would have been time to do something about it. Yet it was discovered that two minutes and eight seconds into the flight the automatic stall recovery system had been switched off. Who made the fatal error? BEA operated an in-flight monitoring system whereby a third man was seated behind the pilot and co-pilot and supposedly able to react to anything amiss. Yet nothing was done and the plane lost speed and height, went into a deep stall and the impact came 22 seconds later. As the painstaking investigations into the mystery continued, it became clear the accident was probably the result of a combination of circumstances that could not reasonably have been predicted. Nevertheless, it resulted in significant changes to the airline's training and operational policy.

At the time, British European Airlines (a predecessor of British Airways) was facing the threat of strike action by pilots in support of a pay claim. The pilot of flight BE 548 was Captain Stanley Key, 51 years old, highly experienced with 15,000 flying hours, including about 4,000 in charge of Tridents. A much-decorated veteran of the Second World War, he was very much 'old school' and opposed to the planned strike. He was unpopular with his colleagues. After the crash, graffiti was discovered in the cockpit. It read: 'Captain Key – God's next representative in BEA'. That this ironic insult had any bearing on the accident is unlikely. There is no evidence that Key ever saw it.

What almost certainly did have an effect was the blazing row about the strike that Key had in the pilots' room at Heathrow shortly before going aboard. He was not a man who hid his opinions and the vehemence with which he put them across must have alarmed his co-pilot, an inexperienced 22-year-old, Jeremy Keighley. No one knew that Key was suffering from a serious but undiagnosed heart condition. Forensic tests later showed that he had suffered a ruptured blood vessel in the two hours before the crash. He would almost certainly have been suffering chest pains before he took off, perhaps passing these off as indigestion.

Under these circumstances he could easily have made an error during the take-off procedure, stressful enough under normal circumstances, let alone if you are having a heart attack. Would Keighley, having witnessed Key's frightening outburst in the pilots' room, have had the confidence to countermand his irascible superior? The author John Withington, writing about the Trident crash in his book *Capital Disasters* (2003), says that Keighley was regarded as 'a promising young man but lacking in self-confidence and with a tendency to be comparatively slow to react'.

Withington points out that the Trident was the first British aircraft to be fitted with droops. There were two similar levers – one for the wing flaps and the other for the droops – where other aircraft had just one. Was it possible that Key pulled the wrong lever and Keighley was unsure what to do? Did Key in his pain and irritation bark out an order that his inexperienced and flustered colleague misunderstood? What was the role of the third member of the crew, Second Officer Simon Ticehurst, whose job it was to monitor the other two? It was suggested that at the critical moment he had been preoccupied with filling in the log. Another pilot was also on the flight deck, Captain Collins, the captain of an air freight plane, who had hitched a ride to Brussels at the last minute. His body was found with an aerosol can of air-freshener in his hand. Could he have been distracting the crew in some way? Ironically, it turned out that the three-man crew had only been on stand-by that afternoon and had been assigned to the Brussels flight because the originally-rostered crew were delayed. Had they not been, it is probable that the crash would not have occurred. If there had not been the airline strike in Europe, the BEA plane would not have been so full.

There was no cockpit voice recorder on the BEA Trident so it was not possible to say with certainty what actually happened. The inquiry concluded that Captain Key's heart condition resulted in a loss of concentration and errors of judgement that were not noticed by his colleagues. As a result he failed to correct the stall and he may have confused the levers, causing the wrong one to be pulled.

Following the Trident crash, cockpit voice recorders (already mandatory on some other airlines) were fitted to all BEA aircraft.

Part of the wreckage of the Trident. (Surrey Herald and News)

The training of pilots was modified to bring in a new emphasis on acting as part of a team, rather than as an autocratic commander in the old tradition.

Thirty-two years later, the townspeople of Staines paid belated tribute to those who had died. In June 2004 a memorial service was held in St Mary's church and a stained glass window unveiled and blessed by the Bishop of Kensington. Among those present was Frances Castledine. Nearby, a memorial garden was dedicated on the Moormede Estate.

The people of Staines came in for a lot of criticism because of the behaviour of the crowds that clogged the by-pass on that awful Sunday afternoon, although some locals claimed that many spectators came from further afield. Perhaps these memorials, suggested by local resident David Macdougald (another helper among the first to get to the scene) and instigated by Spelthorne Councillor John O'Hara, will do something to atone for those shameful scenes.

AVALON IN ENFIELD?

———— ❖ ————

Enfield is not the most obvious place to associate in the mind with the mystic Isle of Avalon but a discovery in the grounds in 1981 seemed to link this suburban district with the legendary King Arthur himself.

There was considerable interest among Arthurian experts when a Mr Derek Mahoney appeared at the British Museum with an inscribed lead cross which he said had been recovered from the bed of the lake near Maiden's Brook in the grounds of Forty Hall. This was no run-of-the-mill archaeological find. Mr Mahoney claimed that it was the very same relic that had graced the coffin of King Arthur at Glastonbury!

Back in 1191 the monks at Glastonbury Abbey had, they said, discovered the grave of King Arthur and Queen Guinevere. On top of Arthur's coffin they found resting an inscribed lead cross identifying the body as Arthur's. A shrine to contain their bones was subsequently built inside the abbey and the monastic community grew rich on the donations of pious pilgrims from all over England. The writer and traveller John Leland saw the cross in 1542 and gave details of its size and description. It was illustrated for the first time in the sixth edition of Camden's *Britannia*, published in 1607. The cross remained at Glastonbury until the abbey was destroyed in 1553 during the upheavals of the Reformation. Its fate after that was unknown, although it is said to have been seen in Wells in the 18th century. This was the unique and precious artefact that Mr Mahoney brought to Bloomsbury.

Or was it? It seemed too good to be true and suspicions

The imposing Jacobean house known as Forty Hall.

deepened when Mahoney refused to leave the cross at the museum for further examination. He had allowed it to be photographed but after that he never showed it publicly again.

Forty Hall is an architecturally important Jacobean house built for Sir Nicholas Raynton between 1629 and 1636. It lies back from the road called Forty Hill in extensive grounds a mile or so north of Enfield town centre. These grounds, including the lake where the cross was said to have been found, were owned by the London Borough of Enfield as a public open space. This ownership enabled them to take Mr Mahoney to court in an attempt to recover the cross. He refused and was sentenced to two years' imprisonment for contempt of court. He was released after serving about half his sentence but not before the affair became the subject of extensive media coverage.

He still asserted that the cross was genuine but by now public interest had waned and he was himself far from well. He had not been able to resolve various legal problems that had been concerning him and eventually he took his own life. The cross was never seen again.

Was it the genuine article? Mr Mahoney did have some circumstantial basis for his claims. It was true that the noted antiquarian Richard Gough, an editor of Camden's *Britannia* in which the drawing of the cross had appeared, had lived locally at Gough Park from 1714 to 1809. He was a great collector of antiquities, just the sort of man to have treasured such a relic. However, there is no mention of the cross in his papers bequeathed to the Bodleian Library at Oxford, nor in the catalogues of his collection, which was sold after his death.

Sadly for those of a romantic disposition, the evidence suggests that the cross was a forgery, made by Derek Mahoney himself. He had been a lead-pattern maker for a well-known local firm of toy car makers and would have had the skills necessary to make a convincing copy. He had been for some time a member of the Enfield Archaeological Society, assisting with Carbon-14 dating and x-raying of iron objects discovered in the society's excavations. Through his interest in local history Mahoney was aware of Richard Gough's antiquarianism, but it is unlikely that the cross could at any time have made its way from Gough's collections to the lake at Forty Hall without some public comment about its loss.

Members of the Enfield Archaeological Society kept a watching brief at the lake while it was being cleaned out and the operator of the dredging machine was known personally to them. He was quite sure that no lead cross had been found.

Local historian Geoffrey Gillam explained to me how he was involved in a couple of television documentaries concerning the fake cross. 'I made a copy of it, just to show how easy it was to do,' he said. 'I still have this cross and it gets an airing every so often.'

Why then did Mr Mahoney go to the bother of making this forgery that was to cause him so much trouble? It seems that he did it in order to get publicity for his long-running legal battles with a firm of solicitors and an estate agent concerning the sale of a house.

The cross was never found and it is believed that Mahoney had destroyed it soon after showing it to the staff at the British Museum, doubtless to avoid the possibility of its being discovered and the hoax exposed. Enfield therefore lost its chance to be linked with Glastonbury, Tintagel and the rest in the Arthurian tourist trail.

It's ironic, really. The original cross was almost certainly a forgery itself, constructed by those medieval monks to enhance their prospects in the lucrative pilgrimage market.

Drawing of the Glastonbury cross from an edition of Camden's Brittania dated 1610.

John White of the Seventh Hussars

❁

Your sons of Great Britain attention pray give unto me for a
while.
Let us hope that on every brave soldier Dame Fortune in
future will smile.
The disgraceful affair was at Hounslow, has excitement great
caused afar,
The death of John White, the brave soldier, of Her Majesty's
Seventh Hussars.

These lines distributed in 1846 by John Harkness of Preston, a prolific printer of Victorian ballads, tell of a horrific case of official cruelty that caused a national scandal and brought about a change in the way the Army treated its recruits. The victim was Frederick John White, who died from the effects of the flogging inflicted upon him at Hounslow Heath by order of a military court martial. The fact that a ballad-printer in faraway Preston thought it worthwhile to produce and distribute the story shows how widespread was the revulsion that the flogging had caused.

John White was a native of Yorkshire, brought up in the
famed town of Leeds.
He had been a policeman and soldier, though scarce in his
prime as we read.
He died by the laws of his country, with his body all covered
with scars.
May never again a brave soldier die the death of John White
the Hussar.

White never denied that he liked a drink, the occasional glass of gin was just what he needed to make army life more bearable – but on 1st June 1846 he had drunk just that little bit too much. On his return to Hounslow Barracks he was shouted at by a sergeant and his temper, always somewhat uncertain by all accounts, suddenly snapped. He grabbed hold of a poker and struck out at the man who had abused him, Sergeant John Darley, catching him a glancing blow across the chest. That was the end of it as far as White was concerned and he collapsed, swearing, onto his bed.

The military authorities did not see it that way. Fifteen days later, after a brief court martial on the charge of striking a superior, White was sentenced to a flogging. This would be the first time he had ever been flogged and at 9.15 am on 16th June, in front of the regiment attired in full dress uniform, White was stripped to the waist, lashed to a ladder in the barracks riding school and flogged by the Farrier Master and his assistant.

*John White was tied up to a ladder, no halberd there was in
    the place.*
*It caused his comrades to shudder. To England it was a
    disgrace.*
*The cat on his shoulders did rattle. The sound it did echo
    afar.*
*Oh, remember the Hounslow battle and John White of the
    Seventh Hussars.*

This was the normal treatment in the army or navy for acts of insubordination. It was savage and brutal and men had died as a result of it being carried out. Public concern had led to military punishments being the subject of a Royal Commission in 1835 but this had concluded that flogging was the only way to keep the lower ranks under control. A description of a public flogging written by Frank Peel in *The Risings of the Luddites* (published in 1880 and quoted by Roy Palmer in *The Sound of History* in 1988) makes it clear just how horrific such punishments could be:

Stepping forward and measuring the distance for an instant

the man raises the whip. It whistles softly through the air and descends on the white back of the soldier on which a broad red line appears, while underneath the muscles quiver visibly. Again and again the whip is raised and descends, and by and by the onlookers are shocked to observe that the skin is broken. The blood begins to trickle slowly down and the sight becomes sickening. The women in the crowd, for there are many present, turn their eyes from the sight, and even stout-hearted men cannot forbear to express their pity for the poor wretch who, with pale face and firmly compressed lips, suffers the dreadful blows.

When his ordeal was over, White – still conscious – was untied from the ladder. A bucket of water was thrown over the shirt that had been put over his bleeding back. Then he was marched the 30 yards to the barracks hospital where his back was covered in wet rags. Here, according to army records, his injuries were deemed not too severe. His back, it was said, was not badly lacerated, 'the real skin not being cut through'. His punishment had, after all, been relatively lenient – only 150 lashes. The writer of the official history of the regiment, C.R.B. Barrett, was later to conclude that 'according to the rules of the service at that date, the amount of punishment was not stated to be excessive'. Yet the wounds were still causing him agony the following day and he also complained of a burning pain in his chest.

He was duly treated and all seemed well until the morning of 6th July, the day on which he was due to be discharged and return to duty. Although his back was, allegedly, completely healed, White now complained of a pain in the region of the heart, through his back and shoulder-blade. Dr Warren, the regiment's surgeon, who had been present at the flogging, did all that he could but paralysis set in and White died on the evening of 11th July. Although the military authorities denied it, many believed that the brutal flogging that he experienced had led to his death.

Certainly his comrades thought so. The historian Harry Hopkins, who described what happened in *The Strange Death of Private White*, published in 1977, said that according to one story that swept through Hounslow in the days that followed, the musket-balls were taken away from the men of the 7th Hussars, lest they shoot Colonel Whyte, the regiment's commanding officer. He received hate-mail from all over the country. One letter, posted in Dublin, accused him of murder and stated that the writer intended to put a bullet in him 'at the next Review'. Whyte flippantly commented at the Coroner's inquest that this letter was very civil compared with many he had received and the only thing that bothered him was that most of the writers forgot to pay the postage! This sort of attitude, typical of officers of the day, did not go down too well, either locally or further afield.

> *Round Isleworth, Brentford and Hounslow and Heston it*
> *caused much pain.*
> *In Twickenham, Richmond and Hampton, in Sunbury,*
> *Egham and Staines.*
> *Thomas Wakeley empanelled a jury, which caused great*
> *excitement afar.*
> *From London resounded to Newry the fate of John White*
> *the Hussar.*

The inquest was held at the George IV inn at Hounslow Heath. It was the way the coronor, Thomas Wakeley, handled this particular case that ensured it would become a cause célèbre and bring about much-needed changes in army practice. He was the editor of the *Lancet* and medically qualified, which was unusual for a coroner in those days. He was also a Radical MP with his own political agenda perhaps. He took the unprecedented step of hearing the evidence of the private soldiers first, instead of the officers, and excluded all but the jury from the court while they were giving evidence. He gave assurances that they could give their evidence without fear of repercussions. This was the first time private soldiers had ever been able to speak freely and publicly about what went on. Their graphic accounts were compelling and by the time the officers involved came to give evidence the jurors' minds were probably made up.

Wakeley also called for an exhumation of White's body and an independent autopsy. This contradicted the findings of the original army death certificate which gave 'inflammation of the lungs' as the cause of death. The new autopsy stated quite categorically that the flogging had brought about his death. Dr Erasmus Wilson, a surgeon at the Middlesex Hospital in London, told the inquest that muscles and flesh around White's spine had been smashed to pulp, causing the fatal inflammation to develop: 'I have no doubt in the world that this man would be alive now had he not been flogged.' It was admitted though that White's liver was extremely enlarged and he would probably have died of drink fairly soon anyway.

The jury unsurprisingly found against Colonel Whyte, who was banished to his family estates in Ireland, and called publicly for the abolition of flogging. Public meetings in Hounslow and other garrison towns repeated this demand. Political turmoil on the Continent and fear of revolution at home led Parliament to reconsider military punishments as a matter of urgency. The maximum number of lashes was reduced to 25 by 1877 and by 1881 flogging had been abolished altogether, except in military prisons where it lingered on until 1907. The death of John White had not been in vain.

The vicar at Heston also played a noble part in this affair. When he had been approached by the military authorities to bury the body without fuss or ceremony, he refused until a post-mortem had taken place. The Army had done all they could to prevent this but he made sure it did. Descriptions of the flayed body featured in the newspapers and ballad printers like Harkness made sure that even the illiterate got to hear of the outrage.

> Then Britons all meet in communion, petition the State and the Queen.
> Be ready, be willing and soon then to banish such disgraceful scenes.
> May flogging be ever abolished at home and in nations afar.
> Nor more let a soldier be punished like White of the Seventh Hussars.

The grave of John White in St Leonard's churchyard, Heston.

John White's grave lies on the north side of Heston churchyard. A headstone was erected in 1977 by Major Jack Sutherland, L/Cpl John Attwood and Mr Cullen, the Museum Orderly, of the 7th Queen's Own Hussars, replacing the original stone that had been broken by vandals. By this action perhaps, however belatedly, the regiment acknowledged their guilt.

Even now the case of John White causes strong feelings. The Preston-based folk group 'Strawhead' who have researched the Harkness material in the last few years (and to whom I am indebted for much of this story) sing this song with a feeling of outrage and anger that takes the listener right back to the grim barracks at Hounslow over a century and a half ago:

Tied up hands and feet to a ladder, while the sound of the cat reached afar.
Oh, Britain, thy deeds make me shudder. Remember poor White the Hussar.

SECOND SIGHT

Unsolicited offers of help from mediums or clairvoyants claiming to be able to solve crimes that have baffled the police are treated by the authorities with considerable suspicion. Sometimes, though, they really are onto something and their information provides the breakthrough in a difficult investigation. The series *Strange But True?*, produced by London Weekend Television, highlighted two intriguing cases.

On Sunday, 24th February 1974 the painting *The Guitar Player* by Vermeer was stolen from Kenwood House on Hampstead Heath. Valued then at two million pounds, it was an unlikely target for thieves as it was so well-known that they could never have disposed of it safely. The police were baffled

Kenwood House, Hampstead.

and the mystery was widely reported in the newspapers and on television.

The motive became clear when a communication was received from the IRA, whose terrorist campaign against the British government had spread to the mainland. 'Nothing is more lunatic,' the message read, 'than that the theft of the painting has received more publicity than the deaths of your soldiers … All we have established is that a capitalist society values its treasures more than humanity. Therefore we will carry our lunacy to its utmost extent. The painting will be burnt on St Patrick's Night with much cavorting about in true lunatic fashion.'

The detectives investigating the case were contacted by Nella Jones, a lady whose Romany ancestry had, she believed, conferred on her the gift of 'second sight'. She had heard about the theft of the picture and was convinced that she could help.

'I saw a vision of the white front of the house,' she said afterwards.

The officers at Hampstead police station were tactful but sceptical. She showed them a map she had drawn which showed the outline of Kenwood, together with two crosses marked in the grounds at the back of the house. One of these crosses, she told them, marked where the frame of Vermeer's painting had been discarded. She was less sure about the significance of the other cross but thought that it marked the position of 'a metal object connected with the theft'.

It all seemed most unlikely and no one was more surprised than the detectives when the picture frame was indeed found where Nella said that it would be. With her credibility restored, Nella was taken to Kenwood to help in the search of the area indicated by the second cross. She had not been to Kenwood before but, according to Detective Inspector Jim Bayes, 'she didn't deviate. She went straight to the pond. It was as if she was drawn there. She said: "There is something very important, connected with the painting, in the pond".'

Wading into the water herself, she bent down and from a depth of about two feet, brought up what turned out to be the metal casing of the alarm system that had been attached to the painting – and which had so signally failed to protect it!

By now some of the police officers were beginning to suspect that Nella knew more about the crime than she was letting on. Should she, in fact, be their prime suspect? However, they quickly established her alibi – there was no way in which she could have stolen the picture herself.

It seems certain that Nella was a genuine psychic. She correctly predicted that there would be several ransom notes received – and that the threat to destroy the painting on the night of 17th March was a bluff and would not be carried out. Finally, following a vision, she was able to tell them that the picture would be found in a cavernous underground hiding place at a cemetery. The nearby Highgate cemetery seemed to fit the bill and it was exhaustively searched – but to no avail. Had Nella's powers finally let her down?

A few days later, the missing Vermeer was found a few miles away – in a cemetery alongside St Bartholomew's hospital! It seems that Nella had been right all along. Neither was it the end to her baffling powers. In the case of the Yorkshire Ripper murders, she correctly predicted that the murderer came from Bradford, that his first name was Peter and that he had already been interviewed by police and released. She was right in every detail.

The second Middlesex case also concerns terrorists. In 1989 Chris Robinson, a Bedfordshire man in his early forties, began to have vivid dreams, premonitions of frightening future events. He would wake knowing that these things were to come but the details were not precise enough to give adequate warnings that the authorities could act upon.

Some of these dreams concerned the RAF base at Stanmore. He visualised wild dogs scrambling through a graveyard, clambering over a fence and turning into people. Once over the perimeter fence, in an area surrounded by photographic equipment, they placed a ticking clock and ran away.

Interpreting this as a warning of an IRA attack, Chris telephoned the base to warn those in charge that an outrage was imminent. Brian Earl, the security officer on duty, took down the details and the call was officially logged. There was not much else that could be done because Chris was unable to say exactly when the attack might happen. Earl also contacted the

Bedfordshire police and established that Chris Robinson was already known to them. He was not a crank, they said. He had already provided them with valuable and accurate information relating to previous crimes.

Chris then decided to drive down to Stanmore to repeat his warnings. He brought with him written records which also confirmed that he had been right in the past. Brian Earl was impressed that he had taken the trouble to come to Stanmore at his own expense. His evident agitation and concern about what might happen seemed genuine enough. His description of his dreams relating to the base showed an awareness of its detail and geography that he could not reasonably be aware of otherwise.

The Commanding Officer of the base was sufficiently disturbed by what he heard to order that the guard be doubled all around the station. However, there was still the problem that Chris Robinson was unable to give a particular date on which the attack

The graveyard of the ruined church at Stanmore, the subject of some of Chris Robinson's vivid dreams.

could be expected. There was a limit to the time for which the increased level of security could be justified. Nothing happened and the extra guards were withdrawn.

Four weeks later a bomb did explode on the base. It was exactly as Chis had predicted. The terrorists had entered the base through a graveyard at the rear of the site. The bomb wrecked the unit's photographic stores, but luckily, no one was injured.

THE SIGNS OF
THE ZODIAC

---------- ✸ ----------

Glastonbury has long been considered the centre of a mystical landscape of immense power and significance. There are many who believe that the outlines of astrological figures can be traced in the field boundaries, lanes and natural features of that part of Somerset. The Glastonbury Zodiac, as this pattern is called, is visible from the air and on detailed maps and covers a circular area roughly ten miles across, centred on the town. The figures vary in length from a mile up to five miles and are in roughly the same positions relative to each other as the constellations are in the sky. Believers in the Zodiac claim that not only are the figures visible in the landscape, but the areas covered by them exhibit the typical characteristics of the star sign.

The Glastonbury Zodiac was first described by Katherine Maltwood in her 1935 book, *A Guide to Glastonbury's Temple of the Stars*, reissued in 1964. Clues in a medieval romance, *The High History of the Holy Grail*, gave her the idea. Parts of this mysterious story are set in Somerset and its anonymous author claimed to have based it on a document found at the Abbey. Whatever the truth of these claims, the Glastonbury Zodiac has been a major element in supporting the hippie New Age culture that sustains much of the spiritual and commercial life in the town.

What is less well-known, perhaps, is that some believe in a similar Zodiac in the district around Kingston, the ancient county town of Surrey. Astrological figures are no respecters of boundaries and the Kingston Zodiac extends over a significant area of South West Middlesex. Kingston's answer to Katherine Maltwood is Mary Caine.

An expert on the Glastonbury Zodiac, she was intrigued when a friend suggested that she might investigate whether a similar phenomenon could be traced around her home town. At first she dismissed the idea but, having noted that some of Kingston's pubs had astrological names such as The Ram, she took things further.

'Taking the hint from Kingston's 'Three Compasses' (now demolished),' she wrote, 'I drew a circle of five miles radius – the size of the Glastonbury Zodiac – from Kingston church. Westward it hit Sunbury's prehistoric boundary mound. The westering sun's setting point? Sunbury Cross was also on it, where several ancient tracks meet. Hanworth Mound, also an ancient crossroads, was a near miss. Syon House, once a Brigittine monastery, was a northern point.'

A promising start, but try as she might, she could not find the outlines of the Signs of the Zodiac within the circle. It was only when the enormous figure of Leo, centred on Chessington, leapt out at her, that she realised that the Kingston Zodiac must cover a much larger area than its illustrious companion in Somerset. It needed a circle some 16 miles across to accommodate it.

Cerberus, *Canis Major*, the dog that guards the Zodiac, together with Leo, Virgo, Libra, Scorpio, Sagittarius, Gemini and Cancer are all on the Surrey side of the Thames – but the others lie in Middlesex, and according to Mary Caine the areas concerned demonstrate the nature of their star signs.

'There is a marked character contrast as we cross Kew Bridge from royal Sagittarius [Kew, Richmond] to busy workaday Capricorn,' she writes. 'Capricorn in astrology is subject to delays and obstructions and motorists attempting to cross this bridge know all about that.' Within the area covered by the figure of the goat, Cassivellaunus blocked Caesar's advance, Edmund Ironside delayed Canute and Prince Rupert defeated the Roundheads, at least temporarily, at the Battle of Brentford.'

The figure appears upside down on the map, its body centred on Ealing with its legs stretching northwards to Acton and Hanwell. It includes Brentford where there is the significantly named Goat Wharf. 'Capricorn works hard for its living and

Kew Bridge, looking towards the Middlesex side.

names like Commerce Road and Occupation Road here proclaim it. You won't find them in Sagittarius.' Chiswick House, Mary Caine points out, was modelled on an Italian original called the Villa Capra – the word capra means she-goat!

The rounded shape of Aquarius can, according to Caine, be read also as the Phoenix-Eagle, or as a waterpot, cauldron or Grail. There is a legend that Edward III gave Osterley Park to a man named Fawkener on condition that he rode round it annually with a falcon on his wrist. 'Why this strange condition?' she asks. 'Did Edward, a great Arthurian, know the Zodiac secret of the Phoenix-Eagle at Osterley and, endeavouring to perpetuate it, give the hill to Fawkener because he had the right name?' Aquarius denotes the rise of the Common Man, she tells us, and two notable owners of Osterley, Sir Thomas Gresham and Francis Child, were both men who rose in status from relatively humble origins to become financiers and bankers of great wealth and influence.

Mary Caine produces a complicated contrivance of old

footpaths, lanes and even a stretch of the Grand Union Canal to demarcate the shape of Pisces centred on Cranford, Heston and Norwood Green. The M4 cuts right across this landscape but apparently lacks any astrological significance. She admits that 'the water-signs all proved the most elusive to find. The Piscean area in the Kingston Zodiac can hardly compete with Glastonbury either with the legends or the clarity of its effigies.' She does her best though, referring to the medieval mural in the church at Hayes which shows St Christopher struggling with the Christ-child through the waves, with fishes and even a mermaid swimming in the waters. Harlington church has a statue of St Peter, the fisherman, with a fish keeping his place in the Bible that he holds.

A characteristic of Pisceans is the tendency to retire from life. Celibacy, Caine says, comes more easily to them – hence the existence before the Dissolution of a monastery at Harmondsworth, whose magnificent tithe barn still remains. 'Even Harmondsworth village has its Piscean qualities, hidden and secluded as it is,' she writes, 'so near the busy Bath Road and the even busier mayhem of London Airport. It keeps its charm unchanged, as if it did not quite belong in the present century at all.'

With its head centred on Hounslow, Aries the Ram is a much more martial star sign, ruled by Mars, the God of War, and the figure includes the areas of Whitton and Hounslow Heath. 'Throughout history armies have assembled on Hounslow Heath,' she points out, 'and Hounslow Barracks is still there, attesting to its long history.' The fearsome Knights Templar owned land locally and one of their insignias was the Paschal Lamb. The name of Hospital Bridge Road recalls the Knights Hospitallers of St John who took over the Templar lands when that Order was suppressed.

Maltwood in her Glastonbury Zodiac assigned Aries to Gawain, the first knight to undertake the Quest for the Holy Grail. Those who know the story will recall that it was his failure to ask a vital question at Grail Castle that caused the Waste Land, when the King sickened, crops failed, women went bald and streams dried up.

Twickenham where Aries and Taurus meet. Sketch by Hugh Thomson in *Highways and Byways of Middlesex*, 1909.

There are not many bald women in the district, but for Mary Caine, 'Hounslow Heath is still a wasteland though largely one of bricks and mortar now – a desert far from deserted. Builders have failed to ask the vital questions and so have created a vast nowhere-in-particular.' Few would argue with her description, I think.

Aries and Taurus meet at Twickenham and she remarks on the transition from Mars (controlling Aries) to Venus (influencing Taurus): 'The Martial aspect applies to the area north of the River Crane which bounds Aries' feet. For Twickenham's old town is on Taurus's head and it is astonishing how immediately the atmosphere changes from Mars to Venus under the graceful influence of the Thames. Charming villages, old church towers and elegant mansions one after another are strung like beads on this sparkling silver cord, from Twickenham through Hampton Court, Hampton, Sunbury, Halliford – where George Eliot and Meredith mused and Thomas Love Peacock swam with Shelley – to Shepperton, a stage set if ever there was one.'

Those of us who live under the shadow of Taurus the Bull might not quite recognise the idyllic Avalon that this description conjures up, but there can be no denying the large numbers of artists and writers drawn to this area: Horace Walpole and Alexander Pope at Twickenham, R. D. Blackmore and Noel

Coward at Teddington and David Garrick at Hampton, to name just a few.

A curiosity of the Kingston Zodiac in this part of Middlesex, which appropriately brings us full circle, is the Little Dog or *Canis Minor*, found just north of the Great Dog's tail at Littleton near Shepperton. Is it a coincidence that Glastonbury's Little Dog is also found at a place called Littleton?

What are we to make of the Kingston Zodiac and Mary Caine's claims for it? Geoffrey Ashe, noted expert on all things to do with Glastonbury, in his book *Mythology of the British Isles*, points out a number of weaknesses in the Glastonbury Zodiac hypothesis and I suppose these could apply equally to the Kingston one. Regarding the Zodiac as 'a modern myth, like ley lines', Ashe contends that 'it involves too many different kinds of feature. It is not formed in any consistent way. Zodiac-finders make use of hills, woods, streams, ditches, roads, hedges, anything that helps.' In such a crowded landscape anyone with a large-scale map, tracing paper and a pen could create shapes that were plausible to the credulous without too much difficulty. Some of the Glastonbury figures are, in any case, simply unrealistic or wrong, according to Ashe. Many have looked at aerial photographs and cannot recognise them – until they are pointed out by a true believer.

The suburbs around Kingston and Twickenham are considerably less romantic in their ambiance than the brooding Somerset Levels. Hampton Hill is hardly Glastonbury Tor. Somehow, I fear that etherial New Agers are unlikely to colonise the district to usher in the Age of Aquarius!

THE UNIVERSAL
PROVIDER

❀

In 1845 William Whiteley, an ambitious young man from Leeds, headed south in search of fame and fortune. He was just 24 and had only £10 in his pocket yet he was destined to establish one of the most prestigious department stores of the Edwardian era – and then to be murdered, at the height of his fame and fortune, by a deranged young man who claimed, perhaps plausibly, to be his own son.

Young William's ambition was to create a department store that could supply literally everything that a customer could want – the first ever one-stop store, in fact. He spent the next six years learning all he could about the retail business and saving his money. By 1851 he was able to open a ribbons and fancy goods shop in Westbourne Grove in unfashionable semi-rural Bayswater.

Westbourne Grove in those days was known as 'Bankruptcy Avenue' because so many shops had failed there but Whiteley had learnt his trade well. By 1875 this little shop had expanded sufficiently to justify its title as 'The Universal Provider'. 'Everything from a pin to an elephant' was its catchy advertising slogan. Whiteley took over adjacent premises and was engaged in ruthless competition. Low prices and special promotions brought the customers in. By 1890 he was employing over 6,000 staff and had bought up farms and factories to keep his store supplied. In 1896 he was rewarded with a royal warrant from Queen Victoria. The public loved him but with his competitors he was very unpopular indeed.

It was perhaps unsurprising that a series of mysterious fires occurred in the 1880s – five in five years, it was said, all put down to arson. The worst was on 6th August 1887. The front wall of his shop collapsed and the inside of the building came crashing down. Four firemen were killed as their engine was engulfed in rubble and twelve were badly injured, as were two policemen. The complex network of gas pipes serving the store was fractured in many places, causing explosions and rushes of flame that the firemen were unable to bring under control. John Withington in *Capital Disasters* (2003) states that the Metropolitan Fire Brigade sprayed more water onto the fire at Whiteleys than on any other fire that they ever fought. The blaze, which had begun at about 7 pm, continued well into the early hours of the next morning. The store was destroyed along with fifteen other buildings.

William Whiteley's total losses came to more than half a million pounds. As a result of the previous arson attacks he was chronically under-insured with cover amounting to only £16,000. Yet such was his drive and determination that the store was rebuilt and trading again within nine months. You couldn't keep an entrepreneur like Whiteley down for very long!

But this self-made man had a fatal weakness. He was a notorious serial womaniser. Some of the young shopgirls in his employ were only too willing to advance their careers by providing additional services after hours, it seems. Among them was Louisa Turner, who was set up in a house in Kilburn in 1882 when Whiteley was 50. At the same time he was said to be having an affair with Louisa's sister, Emily. Emily was then living with a man called Raynor and there was a son, Horace. In later years Horace was to boast to friends that he was the son of a wealthy man. His father could not acknowledge him publicly, he hinted, but one day he would inherit a fortune.

On 24th January 1907 Horace tricked his way into Whiteley's office at Westbourne Grove and confronted him. Shop staff overheard him demanding that Whiteley recognise him as his son and give him his financial due. Whiteley refused.

'Is that your final word?', Horace was heard to shout. 'Then you are a dead man!'

He shot Whiteley in the head and then turned the gun on himself, injuring his hand. He was arrested and put on trial two months later. During the trial he made a number of lurid allegations, not least when he claimed that Whiteley had engaged in what the tabloid press would nowadays dub 'three-in-a-bed sex romps' with Louisa and Emily.

Horace was found guilty and sentenced to death but there was strong support for him from the public. Possibly they believed his stories, or perhaps the revelations about Whiteley's private life had turned people against the victim. Over 200,000 signed a petition for clemency. The Home Secretary granted a stay of execution. Horace Raynor was imprisoned and quietly released in 1919. He died two years later.

Whiteley's store was sold to the Selfridge family in 1927. It entered a period of slow decline after the Second World War – Bayswater was too far from the West End for it to be able to compete on equal terms – and it eventually closed in 1981. The Whiteleys building (relocated in Queensway in 1911) still exists but now houses a variety of different shops.

The former Whiteley's Department Store, now a shopping centre with a range of outlets but retaining the famous name.

MURDER IN THE SUBURBS: THE SEDDON TRIAL & THE BRIDES IN THE BATH

———— ✸ ————

Holloway in the years before the First World War was a respectable middle-class suburb, not the sort of district whose prim residents would wish to be associated with something as unseemly as murder. But in 1912 the proceedings of a sensational trial at the Old Bailey, which kept the newspaper-reading public enthralled for a fortnight, concerned events that occurred at a large family house at 63 Tollington Park, the home of Frederick Henry Seddon, a District Superintendent for an insurance company, his wife Margaret and their five children.

In July 1910 Seddon had let the top floor to a 49-year-old spinster, Eliza May Barrow, her friends Mr and Mrs Hook and a ten-year-old child. It must have been quite congested. Miss Barrow soon fell out with her fellow lodgers and Seddon assisted her in persuading them to leave. She was very grateful to him and she felt confident enough about him to ask his advice on financial matters. She was a wealthy woman, owning several properties including a pub and a barber's shop, as well as having £1,600 in government stocks and over £400 in gold coins.

Frederick Seddon seemed to do quite well out of the arrangement. In October Miss Barrow transferred the government stock to him in return for an annual annuity of £103. Early next year she assigned him the leaseholds of the pub and the shop in exchange for another annuity of £52 a year and the right to live rent-free at No. 63. She seems to have been a very trusting woman, or perhaps Seddon was unusually persuasive.

In September 1911 she fell ill with vomiting and diarrhoea. Her living conditions became very squalid, the room infested with flies. Mrs Seddon got her four arsenic-based fly-papers which were hung around the room. Miss Barrow's condition deteriorated and she made a will naming Seddon as her executor. She died on 14th December. The cause of death was given on the certificate as 'epidemic diarrhoea'.

Seddon did not trouble to inform her relatives of her death. They only found out after she had been buried. They must have had high expectations of inheriting something from her and when they discovered that she had left everything to Seddon, they were furious. Suspecting foul play, they went to the police. Miss Barrow's body was exhumed and discovered to contain suspiciously high levels of arsenic. Mr and Mrs Seddon were arrested and charged with murder.

At the Old Bailey the prosecution claimed that the Seddons had boiled up the fly-papers to extract the arsenic

Eliza Barrow had a flat on the top floor of this house in Holloway.

and administered it to Miss Barrow in her food. Mrs Seddon admitted their purchase of the fly-papers for the sick-room but denied any evil intent. The Seddons' contrasting demeanour in the dock seems to have been a crucial factor in the verdicts reached. Mrs Seddon was quiet, polite and submissive and was acquitted. Her husband, on the other hand, came across as overbearing and conceited. He was found guilty.

There was a strange moment at the end of the trial. Before being sentenced, Seddon made what was described as 'a ritual masonic sign' and announced, 'I declare before the Great Architect of the Universe, I am not guilty.' If this was an attempt to influence the judge, a fellow mason, it failed. 'Our brotherhood does not encourage crime. It condemns it,' he replied and sentenced him to death. Seddon was hanged in Pentonville Prison on 18th April 1912.

Unlike Holloway, Bismarck Road (off Highgate Hill and the Archway Road) was not perhaps the address to have in 1914. Things German were not exactly popular with the British public. There was another reason, though, why the squeamish might prefer to have something different on their letterheads – the association with the notorious 'Brides-in-the-Bath' murders.

Mr Lloyd seemed such a nice gentleman when he rented a flat at No. 14 with his charming young wife, Margaret. So sad then that Mrs Lloyd soon became unwell with dizzy spells and headaches. Dr Bates, the local doctor at his surgery in the Archway Road, could not find anything obvious wrong with her. Whatever it was would soon pass, he thought, and he was shocked when on 15th December he was sent for with the news that Mrs Lloyd had been found dead in the bath. He was forced to the conclusion that another dizzy spell must have overcome her, causing her to lose consciousness and slip under the water.

This tragic 'accident' was reported in the national newspapers and it was this publicity that trapped 'Mr Lloyd' whose name was in reality George Joseph Smith. It brought back painful memories for two other sets of parents who had suffered similar bereavements. Two more young brides, Beatrice Munday at Herne Bay in 1910 and Alice Burnham in Southsea in 1912, had been found dead in their baths, apparently as a result of unexplained fits or fainting attacks. In both cases the husband had left the area soon afterwards.

The father of one of the dead girls had disliked the fellow all along and had opposed the marriage. Questions began to be asked. Smith was exposed as a con man, a swindler and a bigamist whose ploy was to offer vulnerable young women marriage with the intention of getting control of their savings and property.

He seemed to have hit upon a foolproof method, pulling his victims' legs sharply upward while they lay in the bathwater. A police experiment to test this theory nearly killed the young nurse who had foolishly volunteered to play the part of the young bride. Decently clad in a bathing costume she might have been but she nearly died nevertheless!

Smith's mistake, perhaps, was to try the stunt once too often. Yet, despite this, he became almost a hero. It is said that the public gallery at his trial was crowded with young women eager to experience the thrill of being close to such an excitingly wicked man.

George Smith protested his innocence but was found guilty and hanged. Bismarck Road was, much later, renamed Waterlow Road. No. 14 is still there, looking no different from the other houses but hiding a sad secret.

LIFE AND DEATH
OF THE *TELSTAR* MAN

---------------- ❁ ----------------

For devotees of the pop music of the early 1960s, *Johnny Remember Me* and *Telstar* are among the 'all-time great' records. The first, an eerily atmospheric song with lots of echo effects, was a Number One hit for John Leyton in 1961, and the instrumental *Telstar*, played by the Tornadoes, reached the top in both Britain and America a year later. It was the first record by a British group to top the US charts.

The records' distinctive sound owed much to the genius of their producer Joe Meek, who seemed to be at the start of a glittering career in the music industry. Yet, less than six years after the haunting doom-laden *Johnny Remember Me*, Meek was dead, a victim of a bizarre shooting incident in North London where he fatally shot his landlady before turning the gun on himself.

As Amanda Hallay outlined in an internet feature found on the worryingly-named website, www.kittensinunderpants.com, Meek's troubled personality and strange childhood led to a paranoia that tragically overwhelmed his inventive ability. He was born in the small town of Newent in Gloucestershire in April 1929. His mother had, it seems, wanted a daughter and dressed him as one. Apparently he liked wearing dresses but there cannot have been many boys living on the edge of the Forest of Dean at that time who did!

As a child he was fascinated by tape recorders and the sounds they could be made to produce by manipulating the speed or playing things backwards. When he left school a job with the Midlands Electricity Board gave him access to more sophisticated components and technology. He began recording local bands and sending the resulting demo tapes and records to the major recording companies. This led to a job with Radio Luxembourg in 1956 and his first success was a jazz trumpet recording in 1960 which made the lower reaches of the hit parade. It was about this time that Meek moved into a flat above a shop at 304 Holloway Road. There is a cycle shop there now but nothing to indicate that the flat upstairs was once one of the most innovative recording studios in the history of popular music. Many of the most famous recordings made in the infinitely more sophisticated studios at places like Abbey Road – even the Beatles' *Sergeant Pepper* LP – owe a lot to the techniques first dreamed up by Joe Meek.

By today's standards the technology was incredibly primitive. *Telstar* was just one of the classic pop records recorded in, of all places, Meek's bathroom. In six years he produced 245 singles, 45 of which reached the Top 50 in Britain. Other smash hits included *Wild Wind* (another by John Leyton), *Just Like Eddie* (an Eddie Cochran tribute recorded by Heinz) and *Have I The Right?* (The Honeycombs). All seemed to be set fair.

Yet there was a dark side to this tall and handsome man. His fascination with strange sound effects became obsessive and sinister, to the extent of setting up recording equipment in cemeteries in the hope of capturing some sound from beyond the grave. He got deeper into the occult, holding seances in the hope of contacting Buddy Holly whose death in a plane crash Meek claimed to have predicted with a ouija board.

Recording artists learned to fear his violent temper; he was known to fling typewriters and even speaker cabinets about in his rage. On one occasion he is said to have held a gun to the head of drummer Mitch Miller (later a member of the influential Jimi Hendrix Experience). Mitchell was allegedly playing the wrong rhythm and Meek swore at him: 'If you don't play it properly I'll blow your ******* head off!'

Joe Meek was homosexual at a time when this was still an illegal activity in Britain. In 1963 he found himself in court charged with 'importuning for immoral purposes'. Many of the male artists he worked with were aware of this but their interests usually lay elsewhere and they made it clear that music was their reason for associating with him, not anything else. For Meek, his homosexuality led not to sexual fulfilment but to feelings of self-loathing and a fear of imminent scandal. He was implicated in an unsavoury murder case in which the body of a 'rent boy' was found in a suitcase in a Sussex field. 'Although it is extremely unlikely that Joe had anything to do with the murder,' Amanda Hallay comments on the website, 'it is probable that he knew more about it than he wanted to.' It was even whispered that he had fallen foul of the infamous Kray twins and that there was a price on his head.

Joe Meek had a flat above this cycle shop in Holloway Road.

Joe Meek was losing his golden touch. He is said to have turned down both The Beatles and David Bowie. Perhaps it was always the sound that interested him, not the songs. The beat groups that dominated the hit parade from 1962 onwards made his records seem increasingly contrived and gimmicky. One of his artists at the time was the infamous Screaming Lord Sutch. Most of the records he produced in his last days were embarrassing flops. He became paranoid about his rivals stealing his ideas, particularly the increasingly-successful Phil Spector, and would search his studio incessantly for bugging devices. It was believed that he was being blackmailed by former male lovers. He was descending into a darkness no one could penetrate.

Exactly what happened on 3rd February 1967 nobody knows. His landlady at 304 Holloway Road was by then one of the few people who tolerated his increasingly unstable behaviour. Perhaps she, too, began to reject him. For whatever reason, he took a revolver and shot her dead. He then turned the gun on himself.

Joe Meek's tragic story has not been forgotten. In the summer of 2005 *Telstar*, scripted by Nick Moran, opened at the New Ambassadors Theatre in the West End, bringing Meek's talent and paranoia to a new audience.

STRANGE ENCOUNTERS
IN THE
KINGS ROAD

———————— ❖ ————————

No. 217 Kings Road (also known as 1 Glebe Place) in Chelsea is a desirable town house built in 1740 in what was then still a village in rural Middlesex. During much of the 19th century it was the haunt of artists, part of a bohemian creative community that did much to establish the district's reputation.

David and Liz Pettifer purchased the house late in 1978 but work being done on the property meant that they would not be able to move in until the following January. While the alterations were being made their furniture was stored in the basement.

On Christmas Eve a friend driving past noticed that the front door was open. He knew that nobody should be there then so he stopped the car, went back and shut the door. He happened to mention this to the Pettifers some time later and they were puzzled but, as nothing was missing and there seemed to be no explanation, they did not worry about it unduly. Astrid St Aubyn in her book *Ghostly Encounters*, published in 1996, described what happened next.

At Easter the new owners went abroad for a holiday, leaving their tenant, a young female student who rented the basement flat, still living in the house. Alone, she was alarmed to be disturbed at night by the sound of footsteps in the dining room above. Bravely, and perhaps foolishly, she went to investigate. There was no sign of anyone and nothing appeared to have been moved.

As she returned to the basement the phone rang. 'Who is that with you?' her friend asked, apparently hearing someone in the background. 'No one,' she replied, adding jokingly that perhaps whatever it was had been in the dining room.

Soon afterwards Liz Pettifer was talking to a guest in the kitchen when the door was closed deliberately by an invisible hand and they saw the doorknob turn. This so alarmed the nervous young man that he fled the house and never returned. Liz's sister, who claimed to be psychic, found herself mysteriously drawn to the dining room on her first visit to the house and was convinced that there was indeed a ghostly presence in the room.

Mr Pettifer contacted the previous owner about these strange happenings. He was unperturbed. 'You've discovered her, have you?' he laughed. 'Have you heard her dress rustling on the stairs?' Nobody had, but one wonders whether a vendor should be legally obliged to inform prospective buyers of supernatural manifestations before contracts are exchanged!

The young lodger moved out from the basement flat and was replaced by Dermot Kelly and his wife, long-time friends of the Pettifers. On a number of occasions it sounded as if furniture was being moved above their heads in the small hours. They thought perhaps it was David Pettifer, an antiques dealer, rearranging his pieces for an exhibition, but it seemed unlikely that their friend would engage in such activities at such an anti-social hour! When they asked their landlord about these disturbances he assured them that he had been in bed and sound asleep at the time.

It was agreed that if such things happened again they would telephone Mr Pettifer immediately, whatever the hour. Nothing happened for several months but at three one morning the noises started again. Dermot Kelly crept to the phone in the darkness and dialled his landlord's number. No reply – the Pettifers were away and there could be nobody up there!

In the end they just accepted the occasional strange noises from upstairs. But they noted that if they spoke above a whisper while the ghost was at work, it would cease its activities immediately and wait until they were completely silent before starting again. They even claimed to have become a little fond of their unseen companion above.

SHOT WHILE IN THE EXECUTION OF THEIR DUTY

❊

Much political capital is made of crimes committed by those who might be described these days as 'asylum seekers' and there have always been such people desperate for work and acceptance from the community. On 23rd January 1909 there occurred one such example, a bungled robbery that became known as 'The Tottenham Outrage'. I am indebted to Deborah Hedgecock of Bruce Castle Museum, Tottenham, and Janet Harris, author of *Outrage! An Edwardian Tragedy* for details of exactly what happened. There were moments of slapstick comedy but, tragically, also two deaths of innocents who happened to be in the wrong place at the wrong time.

At half-past ten on a Saturday morning, 17-year-old Albert Keyworth was returning by car from a bank in Chesnut Road off the Tottenham High Road, having collected the wages for workers at a nearby rubber factory. Two Latvian exiles, Paul Hefeld and Jacob Lapidus, were lying in wait and armed. They attempted to snatch the cash but Albert put up a fight, as did the driver, who was shot several times but protected from serious injury by his thick motoring overcoat. Another man, a burly stoker from the gasworks, came to their aid and was shot four times, receiving painful injuries. In the confusion Hefeld and Lapidus were able to run off with the money.

The robbers had rather unwisely chosen to stage their attack

PC Tyler. (Bruce Castle Museum)

right outside the police station. Constables Newman and Tyler, hearing the shots, rushed out in pursuit, commandeering the victims' car. Pursued into Mitchley Road, the criminals fired, putting the car out of action. A 12-year-old boy, Ralph Joscelyne, running for cover behind the car, was hit by a stray bullet and fatally wounded.

The chase continued on foot and more shots were fired by the fugitives. PC Tyler received a bullet in the head and fell, dying soon after being taken to hospital. Hefeld and Lapidus were pursued for several miles, crossing the Great Eastern Railway tracks and the River Lea. The robbers were by now being chased by a motley array of armed police, passers-by prepared to have a go, and a party of wildfowlers who had been shooting duck on the Tottenham marshes.

On Chingford Road, Walthamstow, the criminals hijacked a southbound tram. Guns blazing, they leapt aboard as the terrified passengers hid under the seats or jumped off if they could. They forced the conductor to drive on. Meanwhile, the police were commandeering a milk float to continue the chase. When the robbers shot the milkman's horse, the police took over a tram that had been heading north, threw it into reverse and continued the chase down the Chingford Road, firing all the while. The scene was now like something out of a Keystone Cops movie!

On board the first tram, the conductor bluffed Hefeld and Lapidus into believing that there were police waiting to ambush them in Forest Road. They suspected a trap but could not take the risk. They leapt off and ran away towards Hale End on the edge of Epping Forest.

Eventually the fugitives were cornered in a dead-end alley. Their only escape route involved climbing a fence alongside the Ching Brook. This was too much for Hefeld who shot himself as the police closed in. He died three weeks later. Lapidus, who was the taller man, was able to scale the fence and, crossing the fields, he made for a workman's cottage where he barricaded himself in an upstairs bedroom. Realising that his position was hopeless, he too shot himself.

Gun crime is sadly commonplace today but a century ago its rarity caused great shock to the newspaper-reading public, especially when the victim was a policeman. The tragic story of Detective Alfred Young is outlined in *The Good Grave Guide to Hampstead Cemetery*, published by the Camden History Society in 2000.

On 14th July 1915 Young went with Detective Sergeant Askew to a house in Holly Hill, Hampstead, to arrest a lodger named Richard Gorges. Earlier in the day officers had removed a revolver and some ammunition from the house and Gorges was to be taken in for investigation into the firearms offence. What they did not know was that he had a second gun. Confronting the two policemen on the stairs, he shot and killed Young.

Gorges was arrested and put on trial for murder. Doubtless the police and the public felt that his guilt was self-evident and were confident of a conviction and the implementation of the death penalty. However, his lawyers put up a persuasive defence. They claimed that 42-year-old Gorges had suffered from crippling headaches since a severe attack of sunstroke while serving with the army in South Africa. He had a drink problem

Houses in Holly Hill, Hampstead.

and Gorges himself admitted to being an alcoholic and being gripped by what his defence called 'a condition of grave excitement' when under the influence. He had been angered by what he believed was the theft of his other pistol and in the struggle on the stairs to disarm him, his gun had gone off by accident.

The court's verdict that, due to the effects of alcohol, he was not responsible for his actions and therefore not guilty of murder was unpopular with the public. He was, however, convicted of manslaughter, the judge – who perhaps had held different views to the jury – commenting that 'manslaughter is a crime of infinite variety and the variety which the prisoner had committed was near akin to murder'. Gorges was sentenced to twelve years' imprisonment.

Detective Young's funeral was the occasion for a great show of grief and mourning throughout Hampstead. Large crowds gathered at the police station to see the mass of floral tributes and the pavements along the route to the cemetery were lined with mourners. Alfred Young, who was 35 when he died, was laid to rest alongside his wife who had died four years before.

I wonder what today's newspapers would have made of the leniency of Gorges's sentence?

BABINGTON AND OTHER PLOTTERS

———————— ❖ ————————

There is nothing left now of Uxendon Farm near Harrow. It stood alongside the Kenton Brook which flows into the River Brent. The last remains of the farmhouse were destroyed in 1933 when the new branch of the Metropolitan Railway from Wembley Park to Stanmore (now part of the Jubilee Line) was constructed across its site – but Uxendon has its place in English history as the location where a plot to kill Queen Elizabeth I came to an ignominious end.

In the 1580s Uxendon Farm was owned by the Bellamy family. They were Catholics – not aggressively so, they married and were buried in the Anglican church of St Mary at Harrow-on-the-Hill, but friendly with and sympathetic to more militant papists who were working towards the re-establishment of the Catholic faith in England. One of these was Antony Babington, whose name is associated with the last of the attempts to replace Elizabeth with Mary, Queen of Scots.

The prime movers were Babington and Father Ballard, a priest trained in France who landed in England in 1586 under the false name of 'Captain Foscue'. Ballard and Babington recruited a number of others to plot a foreign invasion leading to the release of Mary from imprisonment and the removal and execution of Elizabeth.

Unwisely, the plotters committed their plans to paper in letters that were routinely intercepted. Babington's letters to Mary outlined what was intended and her replies showed that she approved it all, including the killing of her half-sister, Elizabeth. As a result the Queen's Secretary of State, Sir Francis

Walsingham, was aware of their plans down to the smallest detail.

When they knew that they had been betrayed, the plotters fled to the safety of the remote fastness of St John's Wood, then in the depths of the country. According to the historian William Camden, Babington and his friends cut their hair short and 'besmeared and soiled the natural beauty of their faces with green walnut shells'. The woods may have given them shelter and concealment but they could not provide food. Driven by hunger they fled to Harrow where Babington knew they would find protection with their co-religionists at Uxendon Farm. They hid in the hay-barn, hoping to remain safe and undiscovered until the hue and cry had died down.

News of the plot had caused great alarm. All Catholics, especially those living in Middlesex, were seen as potential enemies of the state. Camden recorded how Lord Burghley, travelling to London from the royal palace at Theobalds near Enfield, noted groups of vigilantes in the villages along the road between Edmonton and Tottenham. He was told that they were looking for the conspirators and that one of the suspects was believed to have a distinctive hooked nose.

The government's spies were efficient and the fugitives were not to remain safe for long. The outbuildings of Uxendon Farm were searched and Babington and three others arrested. They were brought to trial on treason charges and executed with all due brutality at Lincoln's Inn Fields. The Bellamys, who had sheltered them, did not escape punishment either. Robert Bellamy fled to Holland, was captured and imprisoned in the Tower of London where he and his elder son died. Young Jerome Bellamy was executed for taking food to the fugitives, knowing that they had intended the death of the queen. His mother was also imprisoned, first in the Fleet Prison and then in the Tower where she too died.

One son, Richard, survived and showed great bravery by continuing to harbour Catholic priests at Uxendon, including the eminent Father Campion and Dr Richard Bristow who lived there as 'Cousin Springe – a poor relation of the family'. His daughter Anne, aged only 17, was imprisoned for her faith. She was then persuaded to reveal the hiding place of another priest,

Father Robert Southwell, who had been in hiding at Uxendon. Richard Bellamy was imprisoned for ten years as a result and died penniless in exile in Belgium, his wife having died in prison. Southwell, incidentally, was eventually canonised and a Roman Catholic school in nearby Kingsbury was later named after him.

White Webbs House at Enfield is also associated with a plot to kill the monarch – this time Elizabeth's successor, James I. The house had been given by Elizabeth to Dr Huicks, her physician. In 1605, at the time of the Gunpowder Plot against James I, it was noted that it had been visited by Guy Fawkes on several occasions just beforehand. Fawkes' wife (a figure almost forgotten by history) was said to have stayed there for a month and heard Mass from a Jesuit priest who had visited under an assumed name.

The house was searched and, according to a report presented to the Royal Council, was found to be 'full of trapdoors and secret passages'. What were described as 'Popish books and relics' were found but no weapons or explosives. The house was demolished in 1790 but for generations afterwards White Webbs Lane was known to the locals as Rome Lane because of its Catholic connections.

Religion continued to be a divisive influence in the nation's affairs and an incentive to kill the monarch. In 1698 there was apparently a Catholic conspiracy to murder King William III in Turnham Green Lane (now Wellesley Road) in Chiswick. A renegade Scot, Sir John Barclay, together with a number of associates planned to assassinate the king as he returned home after hunting in Richmond Park.

The historian Macaulay described the lane at that time as 'a quagmire through which the Royal Coach was with difficulty tugged at a foot's pace'. The 40 or so conspirators were hiding in the King of Bohemia Inn and in the hedgerows beside the lane. The idea was to distract the guards and draw them off near the green, giving Barclay a better chance to get near to King William and kill him.

The plot, however, was betrayed. William postponed his hunting. Some of the conspirators were arrested but Barclay himself escaped to the Continent.

DY'D BY ROME'S REVENG'D FURY

❈

On 17th October 1678 the body of Sir Edmund Berry Godfrey, London magistrate and friend of Samuel Pepys, was found on Primrose Hill. It clearly was not a natural death. His face was badly bruised. There were swellings on his neck and a sword thrust straight through his body. Some said that there was evidence that the sword had been inserted after death and that he had, in fact, hanged himself. Most, however, believed that this noted Protestant had been done to death by Catholics and the incident fuelled the hysteria surrounding the so-called 'Popish Plot' against King Charles II.

Two weeks before, Sir Edmund had heard testimony of such a plot from two informers, Titus Oates and Dr Israel Tongue. They claimed to have evidence of plans for a Catholic uprising, the massacre of Protestants, the overthrow of the government and the replacement of Charles by his Catholic brother, the Duke of York.

They were not very convincing witnesses. Oates, a squat and ugly man, has been described by the historian Christopher Falkus as 'a perjurer by profession who had enjoyed a varied career: at one time as an Anglican clergyman, and at another a Jesuit. At the time he was a good Anglican again, burning with zeal to denounce his former co-religionists'. In this venture he found a willing partner in the frail and studious Tongue whose chief occupation, it seems, was the discovery of Jesuit conspiracies.

A number of Catholic peers were said to be behind the plot which, Oates and Tongue claimed, was backed by the Pope, the King of France, the head of the Jesuits and the Archbishop of Dublin. The king, it was variously claimed, was to be waylaid near Windsor by Irish vagabonds, stabbed by Jesuits, shot in St James's Park and poisoned by the Queen's physician! When the allegations were put before the king he treated the two men with contempt. Charles asked Oates some pertinent question – to which he had no convincing answer – and went off to enjoy the racing at Newmarket!

But when, shortly afterwards, Sir Edmund disappeared from his home, to be found five days later dead on Primrose Hill, people began to believe that there

Primrose Hill – scene of the notorious murder of Sir Edmund Berry Godfrey.

might be something in it after all! Israel Tongue then ingeniously pointed out that the victim's name could (almost!) be construed as an anagram of 'dy'd by Rome's reveng'd fury' and hysteria broke out across London. Catholic houses were ransacked in the search for concealed weapons, 'Popish' books and relics were seized and publicly burned and priests hunted down and imprisoned. Mobs marched in the streets to the shouts of 'No Popery!'

Crowds of Londoners surged up to Primrose Hill to view the scene of Sir Edmund's murder. Before his funeral his body was laid out on display in the street, as the historian G.M.Trevelyan described it, 'in dumb appeal to his fellow Protestants'. More than a thousand mourners heard the bishop preach a sermon demanding vengeance. The Whig government was happy to encourage such feelings to strengthen its hold on political power.

An enterprising cutler manufactured commemorative daggers bearing the inscriptions 'Remember the murder of Edmund Berry Godfrey' and 'Remember Religion'. Three thousand of these were sold in a day as people sought to defend themselves against suffering the same fate. Oates was now a national hero, given a state pension and installed in securely-guarded rooms in Whitehall. An accusation by him was enough to send innocent men and women to the cells of Newgate and other informers joined in the fun.

A petty criminal named William Bedloe denounced a Catholic silversmith named Miles Prance as Sir Edmund's killer. Prance confessed but then renounced his confession, confessed again and then recanted once more. He could produce no alibi but eventually saved himself by admitting his guilt and implicating three other men – Green, Berry and Hill. It was enough to condemn them. Those who were much influenced by such things as the anagram of the victim's full name found significance in the fact that Primrose Hill had once been known as Greenberry Hill!

Charles II had been sickened by the anti-Catholic paranoia and refused to give support to it but neither did he intervene when Parliament deprived all Catholic peers, except the Duke of York, of their seats in the House of Lords and passed a motion declaring that 'there hath been, and still is, a damnable and hellish plot for the assassinating and murdering of the King, and for subverting and rooting out and destroying the Protestant religion'.

It was three or more years before the hysterical turmoil died down. The real identity of Sir Edmund's killers on Primrose Hill remains a mystery. On 6th February 1685 Charles II died. He was succeeded by the Duke of York who became King James II. In May Titus Oates found himself brought to trial for perjury. He was sentenced to be flogged twice through the streets of London, a punishment that was probably intended to kill him but did not. When James II was deposed in the 'Glorious Revolution' of 1688, Oates was granted a small pension and lived out the rest of his days in obscurity.

THE GHOST
AT THE
CHILDMINDER'S

———————————— ✵ ————————————

In the late 1980s psychologist Robin Furman led a team of psychic investigators which includied a microbiologist, a computer consultant and an electronics engineer. Travelling around the country in their 'Ghostmobile', actually a 1959 Austin Princess ex-mayoral limousine, they were, it seems, 'in constant demand to tackle hauntings and paranormal experiences of all kinds'. Their stories were put together by writer Moira Martingale and published in 1991 as *Ghostbusters UK: A Casebook of Hauntings and Exorcisms.* It sounds a bit like a forerunner of those countless television 'makeover' shows.

Mrs Bessie Smith was a childminder in Heston. She was becoming increasingly perturbed by ghostly appearances and poltergeist-like effects in the home. 'All the children had seen grey mist in the house,' writes Martingale, '21-year-old daughter Sharon saw the ghostly mist come through her bedroom wall; a milk bottle top had levitated and travelled across the kitchen; doors slammed and toys were seen to move up and down; a picture disappeared from the wall and was never found and Bessie's son John heard an evil roar from inside a bedroom.'

Disbelievers might well say that all these things sound like quite normal occurrences in a typical disorganized household – 'been there, done that' – but the ghostbusters were intrigued. One of the children Bessie looked after during the day began to ask who was the small strange girl she saw in a particular room. When a local clergyman had been called he had allegedly left 'white-faced and in a hurry' after going upstairs and having a bedroom door slammed in his face.

The Ghostmobile duly rolled up outside the Smiths' semi-detached house in a quiet cul-de-sac (or at least a cul-de-sac as quiet as any that close to Heathrow could be). Both Bessie and Sharon are described by Moira Martingale as 'chubby' and, as the family were all heavy smokers, the television (which seemed to be left on permanently) was seen indistinctly through a blue haze. There were clocks everywhere: a cuckoo clock, an ornate brass pendulum clock, a two-foot high Mickey Mouse clock and 'another with a black face which showed a small gold aeroplane going round, displaying the time in most countries of the world'. If there were any ghosts in that little Heston semi, they would have no excuse for not knowing the time!

Mrs Smith told the ghostbusting team that nine years before, when Sharon was only twelve or thirteen, they had called in exorcist, Robert Petitpiere, to deal with strange manifestations that were troubling them. Things had quietened down and they had had no problems for nearly ten years – but now the footsteps and thumps were back once again.

Referring always to the ghost as 'she', Bessie described how bedrooms went cold, apples moved in the fruit-bowl and Sharon's soft toys were left on the floor as if someone had been playing with them. Son John had seen his trainers going up and down in the air and milk had been moved in the fridge by unseen hands. Things were worse when visitors were in the house. 'She doesn't seem to like strangers,' Bessie observed. 'I'm sick and tired of this ghost. She's inconvenient.'

Sharon and Philip, another son, had both seen the ghost. 'I walked through it and so did Philip,' Sharon said. 'It was like a grey mist on the staircase and it made me feel ill and tired. It seemed to come through the wall into my bedroom and once I saw the bedclothes become flat in one spot as if someone had just sat down.' Other incidents were described, including footprints found on a pillow and levitation of Christmas tree baubles. It sounded like a very active ghost indeed.

The ghostbusters set up their scientific equipment, somewhat distracted by Sharon claiming that an ashtray had moved across the table of its own volition. A 'cold spot' was found in the lounge, close to the window – which was odd as the house had double-glazing. As they were packing up later in the evening a sudden crash from upstairs registered on their recording equipment.

As in the famous Enfield Poltergeist case of 1977, the investigators came to the conclusion that the disturbances were somehow centred on the daughter. 'Sharon is a very nice girl,' Robin Furman said, 'but there was clearly some emotional tension there, illustrated by her heavy smoking and weight problems. A lot of confused strong emotions that have not managed to find a suitable outlet so it comes out in this mental or paranormal way. I believe that the way to tackle

Heston churchyard.

this haunting would be to have some beneficial therapy for Sharon, possibly even removing her from the house for a while.'

Sharon's journey home from work took her through a graveyard close to the house. Near the entrance there was the grave of a young girl. Had she, Furman wondered, somehow drawn the spirit of a child close to her? Sharon, even at 21, had a passion for cuddly toys. There must have been a couple of hundred of them piled up on every available surface in her bedroom. No wonder they sometimes seemed to have moved around!

'One hypothesis would certainly be that Sharon may have been drawing external psychical effects to herself,' he concluded. 'When Sharon got home these energies did not get less but they increased because the house was full of children, enabling the little girl ghost to feed upon the energy, encouraging her to remain in the house and manifest more strongly. If you were the ghost of a little girl, is it not conceivable that you might enjoy being in a place where there are many small children and plenty of toys?'

It was difficult to tell what Sharon made of all this. One moment she would say she was 'not bothered' about the ghost, at other times she would say that she wanted it to go. She was puzzled by it rather than frightened. Her mother wanted it eliminated and hoped that the 'experts' would be able to do this – but they could offer no such simple solution.

THE PRESENCE OF PRIMROSE HILL

In 1967 the Society for Psychical Research received a request to investigate strange happenings at a Victorian house at Primrose Hill in North London. Various people staying at the house had reported being disturbed by a mysterious 'presence' in one of the bedrooms. In the most alarming of these incidents one unfortunate man had, apparently, been pulled out of bed and had seen the ghost of a short bald old man, very broad in stature but with an unusually small head. In the circumstances, this seems a very exact description to be able to give of one's attacker!

Even more curious was the fact that this particular malevolent spirit was a creature of very regular habits. The visitations were, it seems, always at three o'clock in the morning and exactly four weeks apart.

Peter Underwood of The Ghost Club in his book, *The Ghost Hunters*, published in 1985, described what happened next. The Society sent John Cutten, one of its most experienced investigators, who volunteered to spend a night alone in the haunted room to record what happened.

If the ghost adhered to his timetable, his next appearance was due on Monday, 20th March. Cutten duly took up residence in the bedroom concerned and locked the door. He sealed it, together with the keyhole and window, in such a way that it would be very obvious if they were tampered with. He rigged up a cotton tripwire that would set off an infra-red camera if it was touched and linked this camera to a thermostat so that it would take a picture if the temperature in the room fell suddenly, another potential indicator of ghostly activity.

Looking across London from Primrose Hill. Ghosts and supernatural happenings occur in the most modern of cities!

He also set up an ordinary camera with flash that he could operate without moving from the bed. A similar mechanism would enable him to switch on a tape recorder automatically at the first sign of anything odd. This ghost, if he did indeed make an appearance as scheduled, would not go unrecorded!

Cutten planned to wake well before 3 am, but in the event he very nearly overslept. He need not have bothered though. Nothing happened at all and frequent checks on the equipment revealed that not a sound or the remotest whisp of anything supernatural had been recorded – quite an anti-climax for all concerned!

Ian Wilson, who refers to this case in *In Search of Ghosts* (1995), makes the best of this disappointment: 'If the residents at the house, perhaps for the sake of sensationalism, had tried to fake a ghostly appearance for Cutten's benefit, then his careful methodology should have picked this up. Indeed, if a hoax had been intended, it might be that the would-be pranksters abandoned their attempt once they realised what they were up against.'

On the other hand, perhaps the old man was camera-shy and decided to haunt elsewhere!

SPONTANEOUS
COMBUSTION

❖

The *Fortean Times* is a journal that recounts strange and inexplicable phenomena from around the world. Among the most frightening of these is the so-called 'spontaneous combustion' of unsuspecting people or even animals.

One of the most curious tales covered by the paper is that of Peppi, a much-loved cat who lived at the Anmer Lodge old folks' home in Stanmore. It reported how one day in November 1986, Peppi was having his usual nap on a chair in the day room when he appeared to be at the centre of an explosion.

'There was a terrific bang and a flash,' said Deputy Matron Irene McSweeney, 'and Peppi flew several feet into the air.' Some witnesses said that the cat was 'enveloped in a blue flame'.

Fire Brigade investigators were called but could find no obvious cause for the explosion. All they could suggest was 'a build-up of static on the cat's fur' but surely that is quite a common occurrence and one that does not normally have such drastic consequences.

I do not know whether Peppi survived this alarming experience. I hope he did – after all, he should still have had eight lives left!

A similar experience unnerved Paul Hayes, a 19-year-old computer operator who, according to the *Fortean Times*, burst into flames as he walked along a quiet road in Stepney Green on the night of 25th May 1985. The upper part of his body was on fire as if he had been doused in petrol and set alight. 'It was indescribable,' he told the *Evening Standard* a few days later. 'My arms felt as if they were being prodded by red-hot pokers. My cheeks were red hot and numb. My chest felt as if boiling water had been poured over it. I thought I could hear my brains bubbling. I thought I was dying.'

He put his hands over his eyes and tried to run to get out of the flames but they followed him and he fell onto the pavement. Suddenly his ordeal was over. The smoke and flames had gone. Yet the burns all over his body were real enough. Luckily he was only just round the corner from the London Hospital. He managed to get to Casualty where he received much-needed treatment.

Paul was lucky – one of the few survivors of the nightmarish mystery that is spontaneous combustion.

MURDER
AT THE
HUSTINGS

———————— ✤ ————————

Eighteenth century parliamentary elections at Brentford were noisy and violent affairs noted for their disorder. Before the 1832 Reform Act, the House of Commons was made up of members elected by the towns (including the so-called 'rotten boroughs'), by the universities of Oxford and Cambridge and by the counties, such as Middlesex. The only people entitled to vote in the county elections were men who owned freehold property worth 40 shillings or more per year. The elections took place at sessions of the County Court and from 1701 this was at Brentford.

In March 1768 the notorious radical agitator John Wilkes was one of the candidates and his slogan 'Wilkes and Liberty' was heard in the streets around The Butts. He was elected, along with George Cooke, to serve as one of the two MPs for Middlesex and his jubilant supporters followed him up to London, allegedly rioting and causing considerable havoc in the capital.

This disorder would have been most unwelcome to the more fastidious Cooke, a Tory who had represented Middlesex since 1750. Perhaps it was all too much for him for he died in June of the same year and a by-election was called to fill the vacancy. Wilkes' friend and lawyer Serjeant Glynn was put up to stand against William Beauchamp Proctor, a Whig who had represented the county since 1747 until coming only third in the poll back in March.

The Butts, Brentford, once the scene of noisy and violent electioneering.

King George III and his ministers had been thoroughly unnerved by the mob hysteria whipped up by John Wilkes and were anxious that the less threatening Proctor should be victorious. Polling day (8th December) was a disaster. That afternoon thugs, armed with heavy sticks and clubs, began a riot, knocking down any who got in their way. Polling booths and ballot papers were destroyed and fighting continued in the lanes and back alleys of Brentford. Shops and inns were damaged as the violence continued.

Eventually the votes were counted and Glynn was declared the winner, polling 1,542 votes to Proctor's 1,276. He was not magnanimous in victory, accusing Proctor of inciting the rioters as it became clear that he was losing: 'at a signal letting loose upon the peaceable, unarmed and inoffensive freeholders of the county of Middlesex in order to destroy those who they could not corrupt and to wrest from them by violence that freedom of election which every undue and constitutional interposition had failed to overthrow.' An enquiry was held at which one witness claimed that he had been threatened by a group wearing Proctor's favours who said that they had no votes but held in their hands weapons that were just as good. Proctor, meanwhile, counter-claimed that the most dangerous rioters were in Wilkes' pay.

During the riot George Clarke, one of Wilkes' supporters, was hit on the head and he died some days later. At first the cause of death was officially given as 'fever' but a surgeon, John Foot, who carried out a post-mortem told the inquest that Clarke's death was undoubtedly due to the head wound. The jury brought in a verdict of 'wilful murder by some person or persons unknown'. A few weeks later two men, Laurence Balfe and Edward McQuirk were charged with the murder, found guilty and condemned to death.

It was then that the government's 'spin-doctors', as we might call them today, set to work. Foot was summoned to meet four eminent surgeons led by John Ranby, formerly principal surgeon to George II, who asked him to reconsider whether, in his opinion, Clarke might have recovered if he had received prompt treatment for the wound. Foot said that he might have and Ranby asked him, as a personal favour to him, to put this in writing. He promised that he would only show this to two or three people but soon it became common knowledge that Foot had altered his opinion. A specially-convened commission of the Surgeons' Company (of which Ranby was Master) announced that Clarke had not died as a result of the blow to the head. A pamphlet was published, entitled *The Blow, or Inquiry into the Cause of Mr Clarke's death at Brentford*, which stated that blood-poisoning from a badly dressed wound was the actual cause of death. Balfe and McQuirk were freed and Foot was left feeling indignant that he had been manipulated by his superiors.

As the two men were known villains who had been involved in similar trouble at previous elections, it seems odd that the powers-that-be were keen to exonerate them. A possible explanation is that the riots had been orchestrated by agents of the state, keen to discredit Wilkes, Glynn and their fellow radicals. Could there have been some sort of shady deal, a promise of eventual pardon for those hired hooligans who carried out the government's dirty work?

LAYING LOW THE LAVENDER MAN

---·❉·---

John Steel was a successful grower of lavender for the perfume trade. He had a shop in Catherine Street off the Strand. Lavender was often used to give a scent to unrefined soap and, as a supplier to the Prince of Wales, Mr Steel found that his business was flourishing.

Like many a city dweller he hankered after the country life and in 1802 he purchased land in the little village of Feltham, with land for lavender growing, and to build a distillery. On 5th November he travelled down there to make sure all was in order for his wife to move in the next weekend. He stayed overnight and the following evening announced his intention of walking across the heath to Hounslow to catch the coach back to London.

He may have had a rosy view of the security of life in the country but his servants decidedly did not. Mindful of the evil reputation of the heath for footpads and highwaymen, they implored him to stay one more night and travel back in the morning – but Steel was adamant. Donning a borrowed heavy coat and taking a sword-stick with him, he set off into the gloom of the November evening.

Somewhere along the main Staines road he was attacked by three ruffians and robbed. His pockets were emptied, his boots and sword-stick stolen. One of the blows to the head that he had suffered proved to be fatal. His body was dumped in a ditch beside the road, close to a milestone.

When he failed to arrive home as expected, a member of his family set off for Feltham to see what had happened. Enquiries were made at Hounslow Barracks and a squad of soldiers was sent to search the heath. The body was soon found, together with bloodstains on the road.

It was not until four years later that a known ne'er-do-well named Hansfield made the mistake of appearing in the town wearing a fine pair of expensive boots that he could never have obtained legally. Under interrogation by the police he admitted that he had been one of the men who had robbed the unfortunate Mr Steel. Turning King's Evidence to save his skin, he named the other two as Holloway and Haggety, alleging that it was Holloway who had bludgeoned Steel to death. Both men vehemently denied the charges but, after a long trial, they were found guilty and sentenced to hang.

The case had generated enormous interest locally and an estimated 20,000 people turned up outside Newgate Prison on Monday, 23rd February 1807 to witness the public executions. They clambered onto any possible vantage point to get a better view. Some got up on an old cart but it collapsed under their weight, pitching them into the crowd where they

The murder of John Steel as depicted in a contemporary pamphlet (courtesy of Eddie Menday).

were crushed underfoot by the crowd surging forward. In the chaos that followed it took half an hour or more to clear the area and to get help to the injured. Twenty-four men, three women and two boys were killed, belated victims of that mugging on Hounslow Heath.

The house that must have had such bitter memories for the widowed Mrs Steel is no more. A Victorian replacement, now used by Age Concern, stands on its site in Harlington Road, Feltham, but the original coach house is still there.

THE MYSTERY
OF
CAESAR'S CAMPS

———— ❈ ————

The earthworks were a mystery to the inhabitants of the villages scattered around the edge of Hounslow Heath. A large square of land was enclosed by a ditch and a bank that must have been taller and steeper when it was new in the time of their ancestors but which was still a prominent landmark in the flat heathland.

In times gone by the superstitious had thought it was the work of the Devil himself and many feared to go there alone or at night. By the more rational days of the 17th century it was recognised that, whatever the structure was, it owed its origin to man rather than some supernatural cause. On Moses Glover's map of the Hundred of Isleworth, drawn in 1635, a note stated that 'In this Heathe hath many camps been pitched: whereof the form of two yet in parte remayneth.'

Antiquarians of the 18th century were fascinated by these remains, still noticeable features of the landscape. It was Stukeley who in 1723 identified one of them as a Roman encampment, giving it the name Caesar's Camp, although he gave no reason other than that it was a Roman site. He measured it out, describing it as 'nearly perfect and sixty paces square'. Lysons, writing at the end of the 18th century put it more exactly – 300 foot square.

Whatever it was, it continued to be shown on maps, such as Rocque's map of Middlesex (1764) and the map that went with the Inclosure Act for the parish of Harmondsworth in 1819. When the old open fields were reorganized, however, following this Act of Parliament, the earthwork was ploughed flat although traces still remained in the soil.

It was only in 1944 that this enigmatic relic was properly investigated by archaeologists. Excavations prior to the construction of the main runway of the new London Airport revealed that it was far more ancient and significant than had been expected. The experts identified the sites of twelve huts and the remains of a temple which they dated to between 500 and 300 BC. So it had nothing to do with Julius Caesar after all.

Curiously, a second archaeological feature not far away was also known by the same name – as far as our forebears were concerned, Julius must have got about a bit! It was on the site of Matthew Arnold School on the eastern side of Staines. The ramparts had long gone but it could be seen from the air as crop marks, especially in dry summer weather. It too was described and illustrated by Stukeley who gave its position as 'on Greenfield Common between Ashford and Lalham'. Again, Stukeley called it Caesar's Camp and wrote that it was bounded on the east by a brook 'which runs into the Thames by his camp at Shepperton'.

Stukeley and other antiquarians at the time believed that it was at Cowey Stakes at Shepperton that Caesar's armies successfully crossed the Thames in their invasion of Britain – but that leads us to another mystery: Where did Caesar's army cross the Thames?

Past generations of pupils studying Latin will have struggled to translate obscure passages in Caesar's *Gallic Wars* in which the great man described his military campaigns in what later became France. In 55 BC his forces invaded Britain, using the time-honoured excuse that it was to maintain peace – the native Britons had been giving support to their kinfolk in Gaul who were still resisting Roman rule.

Bad weather forced him to retreat but he was back in 54 BC with more ships and a larger army. Beating off the hostile British tribesmen, Caesar led his troops northwards towards the valley of the Thames. We know from his account that they forded the river despite stiff resistance. But where?

'The river is fordable at one point only and even there only with

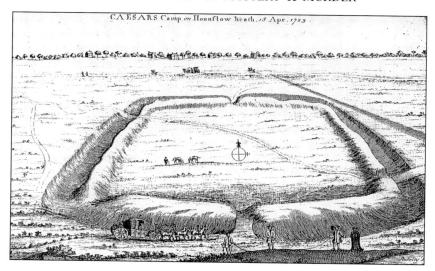

Caesar's Camp as sketched by Thomas Stukeley in 1723. (London Borough of Hillingdon)

difficulty,' Caesar wrote. He went on to describe how the British were lined up on the opposite bank, protected by a wooden fence to which sharpened stakes were attached. There were more concealed under the water. These stakes were described by the monastic historian Bede 800 years later as being 'as thick as a man's thigh, covered with lead and made fast in the bed of the river'. Caesar's army rushed the ford without waiting for low tide and turned the British out of their camp. After pausing to receive the submission of some local tribes, the Romans marched on past present-day Stanmore, being harried by British skirmishers in chariots. Their capital was near what was to become St Albans and it fell to the Romans in late summer.

But did any of this happen at Shepperton and did Caesar indeed have a camp at Staines? Over the years a number of other possible sites for the river crossing have been suggested, including Brentford, Sunbury, Chelsea, Petersham and Isleworth.

According to local historian Valerie Brooking's *Shepperton*

Story (1988), two features which supported Shepperton's claim were the Cowey Stakes themselves and finds of human bones in War Close (now Manor Park). However, as far back as Lysons in 1795 some have claimed that the stakes were simply the remains of a fishing weir. The river has changed its course at Shepperton many times over the centuries. The stakes were found in a spot that would have been about a quarter of a mile north of the river in Roman times. They were at right-angles rather than parallel to the river banks as you might expect. It seems probable that the stakes could have marked a passage through which cows could cross the river safely to pastures belonging to the parish of Shepperton but now cut off by the new course of the river. Cowey could simply be a corruption of 'cow way'.

Stukeley's book *Itinerium Curiosum* (1723) includes a print captioned 'Prospect of Caesar's Camp at Sheparton'. It is not very accurate but seems to show houses and fields across the river from the present Manor House. It was here that the battle between the Romans and the Britons is supposed to have taken place. Stukeley reported that 'spears, swords and quantities of bones' had been found a few years before: did they date from 54 BC or some later skirmish, perhaps involving Viking raiders coming up the Thames? However, later researchers from the London & Middlesex Archaeological Society identified the site as a Saxon burial ground.

Those who put up the monument outside Brentford County Court, however, had no doubts on the matter. 'At this ancient fortified ford,' it reads, 'the British tribesmen under Cassivellaunus bravely opposed Julius Caesar on his march to Verulamium.' This claim is based on the positive identification by Montagu Sharpe in his book *Middlesex in British, Roman and Saxon Times*, published in 1919. He was told by a contractor who had worked on the river bank at Brentford in the previous century that an arrangement of timbers and stakes, just as described by Caesar, could still be seen at that time. Ten feet below the top of the bank was a triple line of oak piling through which was thrust a line of sharpened stakes pointing out at an angle of 45 degrees.

Unfortunately, these details could no longer be checked as the timbers had been removed because they had become a danger to barges using the river for trade. What they were and how old they were can only be speculated on but, if they were what Montagu Sharpe claimed them to be, their removal was an unparalleled act of archaeological vandalism. All that survived was one stake, apparently reused in the construction of a hut in the Romano-British era and discovered in an excavation at Syon Reach in 1928.

However, as at Shepperton, the timbers could have been the remains of a much later weir or protection of the bank against erosion. Gillian Clegg in *Brentford Past* (2002) reluctantly concludes that Brentford is unlikely to be the correct site because, in *Gallic Wars*, Caesar wrote that he crossed at the first possible fording point. Coming from the direction of Kent, that is likely to have been at Westminster, a site known to have been a ford a century later when the Emperor Claudius's forces succeeded in conquering the whole of England.

Construction work on Matthew Arnold School, Staines began in 1938 but was halted on the outbreak of the Second World War. A local newspaper report on the opening of the school in 1954 stated that building plans had to be altered when 'the camp was discovered', though this seems unlikely as it had been known to Stukeley two centuries before.

Any likelihood that Julius Caesar himself once strode across the school playing fields was dispelled by archaeologists from Surrey County Council in 1990. They were able to show that the 'camp' was constructed not in Roman times but in the 12th century AD. The ditches were then filled in during the 14th century, leaving a dip in the soil as the fill settled. Four hundred years later, Stukeley was still able to see the depressions in the ground.

There is still a mystery as to what this enclosure was used for. Access would have been by wooden bridges over the ditches but there was no evidence for any buildings inside. It could have been to keep cattle overnight on their way to market but it seems too strongly constructed for that. It could perhaps have been an official meeting place for the 'moot' or assembly of the leading men of the Spelthorne Hundred, akin to the Borough Council offices just along the road at Knowle Green. Its location close to the meeting point of three parishes – Staines, Ashford and

Laleham – and alongside the main road to Kingston suggests that this might be so.

It would seem that Julius Caesar never had any connection with either of the 'Caesar's Camps' in West Middlesex. In fact, as Julia Gibbs of Spelthorne Museum has pointed out, in the vast majority of cases earthworks known as Caesar's Camp and assumed to be Roman – of which there are many around the country – are prehistoric and date back to well before the Roman invasion. In this respect the example at Matthew Arnold School is unusual in being medieval.

THE GRAVE
OF BOADICEA

———————— ❁ ————————

Harry Potter fans will know all about the significance of platform 9¾ at King's Cross station. What is now less well-known is that underneath platform 10, some would have you believe, lies the grave of Boadicea, the Warrior Queen.

Boadicea, or Boudicca as the experts prefer to call her these days, is one of our national heroes but, I suspect, someone who would have been demanding company in real life. Not that she did not have a great deal to put up with. Queen of the Iceni tribe in Norfolk, she entered history after the death of her husband Prasutagus, who had tried to keep some independence by toadying up to the Romans as a client king. The Romans took the view that now they could take charge of the kingdom and the royal possessions. These, they felt, included the persons of the queen herself and her daughters. Boadicea was flogged and her daughters raped.

The resulting revolt led by the abused queen involved the Iceni and their neighbours to the south, the Trinovantes. The fledgling Roman settlements of Camulodunum (modern Colchester) and Verulamium (St Albans) and even Londinium itself were attacked and destroyed. Each rebel success was celebrated with wild orgies, massacres and human sacrifices. Thousands died, not only Romans but those native Britons who had accepted Roman rule and just wanted to live out their lives in peace.

In the following year, 61 AD, the Roman governor Suetonius Paulinus, who had been away in Anglesey fighting the Druids, assembled a Roman army of 10,000 men and was able, by good use of strategy and military tactics, to defeat Boadicea's warriors.

Where this decisive battle took place is not known; probably it was in the East Midlands but the historian Lewis Spence claimed that it was closer to London and that Boadicea's last stand was on the future site of King's Cross station.

The Warrior Queen got about a bit though – Stonehenge is also claimed as her burial place, her ghost apparently haunts the ancient earthworks of Ambresbury Banks in Epping Forest and, according to the writer Geoffrey Ashe, she has been seen driving her chariot out of the mist near Cammeringham, in Lincolnshire. And others will tell you that she lies deeper into Middlesex, under a mound in Parliament Hill Fields, Hampstead. She would have a better view of London if she was up there.

In Parliament Hill Fields, between the Viaduct Pond and Highgate Ponds, stands an ancient tumulus of uncertain origin. This was excavated in November 1874 in an attempt to prove the persistent local legend that it was indeed here that the Warrior Queen lies. The dig was carried out by workmen employed by the London County Council. Sadly, nothing more was found than an old musket bullet (which clearly was not fired by Iceni rebels or

The tumulus at Parliament Hill Fields.

Roman soldiers) and an 11th-century Indian coin that got there who knows how.

In the book, *London – The Northern Reacher*, Robert Colville described the site as he saw it in 1951. 'Old prints show the tumulus unencumbered save by some tall trees,' he wrote, 'but now an iron rail has been placed around it, and broom and gorse, ancient hawthorn trees, oaks and firs surmount its crown. Round about are a hundred allotment plots with their unseemly concomitant of rejected household utensils, and on top of the summit rests a collection of goalposts. But seen from the top of Parliament Hill or from Ken Wood this tumulus can create its own authentic atmosphere.'

How much British and Roman blood was spilled in the fields and woods of what was to become Middlesex we shall never know – or whether Boadicea does indeed lie within its old boundaries.

It's worth following in her footsteps though. Walk up from Gospel Oak station, as I did one June afternoon in 2004, and look back at the magnificent panorama over London, from Canary Wharf in the east to Westminster, the London Eye and beyond. The tumulus takes a bit of finding, a mile or so across the heath towards Hampstead. A circle of trees, fenced off and raised a little above the path that runs alongside, it looks rather different from how Colville described it in 1951. There are no allotments and no goalposts. In fact I was beginning to wonder whether I was in the wrong place entirely. But then, that all adds to the mystery, doesn't it?

JOANNA SOUTHCOTT'S BOX

❈

'In a small cottage on the Staines Road which was pulled down only about five years ago,' wrote R.S. Cobbett in *Memorials of Twickenham* in 1872, 'lived and preached Joanna Southcott, the deluded Devonshire woman who claimed to be an inspired prophetess.'

A hundred years later her name was still familiar through the frequent newspaper advertisements urging the Bishops and other national leaders to assemble together to 'Open Joanna Southcott's Box'. Who was this strange woman and how did she come to have a devoted following in Middlesex?

She was born in 1750 on a farm in the picturesque village of Gittisham, hidden away in the East Devon countryside near Honiton. Her childhood was unremarkable – domestic service and devout attendance both at the parish church and the Wesleyan Methodist chapel. In her teens she came under the influence of a travelling preacher and visionary who convinced this simple girl that she had the gift of prophecy.

She was prone to 'hearing voices', guided by 'the Spirit of Truth'. The Methodists found her increasingly difficult to deal with and threw her out after she suffered a fit during a bible class and announced to all and sundry that 'God is working out His will through me. I am to become The Lamb's Wife.'

'At first,' said Arthur Mee in his *King's England* volume on Devon (1938), 'she confined herself to weather forecasts and political changes. These being discredited, she formed the habit of writing down her predictions, sealing them and leaving them to await events. Her failures unnoted, her happy hits were magnified, and when she was 42 she publicly acclaimed herself divinely guided in foretelling the future.' 'The Lord,' she claimed, 'has visited me to warn of what is coming upon the whole earth.' She wrote down the revelations she received, keeping them in a strong wooden box.

She became a national celebrity, publishing predictions and moralising in doggerel verses. Travelling around the country, she spoke to large gatherings of poor people who were only too willing to believe her message. Believers were 'sealed in' to become one of the 144,000 who, according to the Book of Revelation, would be saved at the time of Christ's Second Coming. Protection from the Devil could be guaranteed for those who purchased her 'scrolls', actually folded papers sealed with red wax.

Joanna moved to London in 1802 and some time after that began her association with Twickenham. The cottage in which she is believed to have lived for a time was next to a nursery and almost opposite the perhaps appropriately-named Gothic Road. Meetings may have taken place in the cottage or in an adjacent building which was fitted out as a chapel.

By 1809 there was another chapel belonging to the sect by now known as the Millenarians or Southcottians in Middle Lane, Teddington. This prospered and, according to local historian P. D. Barnfield, the worshippers attending came not only from Teddington and Twickenham but also Whitton, Hampton, Isleworth, Barnes, Mortlake and even Andover in Hampshire. They were all from the poorer classes, many living in hovels around the Clarence Arms beerhouse and the green. In 1811, however, the minister left the area and moved to Dawlish. The chapel closed the following year but most of its members joined a new congregation in Twickenham.

Joanna's outpourings became more peculiar. Having abandoned the Methodists, she appealed to the Church of England bishops to test her miraculous powers. At the age of 64 she announced that she was about to become the mother of Shiloh, the second Messiah, 'by the power of the Most High – a man child that is to rule the nations by a rod of iron'.

Amazingly, she was believed and a large house was bought for the birth, while £200 was spent on an ornate cradle worthy of its future occupant and another £100 on nursery equipment. But Joanna was not pregnant with any child, least of all the new Messiah. In fact she was dying of dropsy and succumbed in 1814. An autopsy showed no sign of a baby.

Joanna was buried in St John's Wood cemetery on 1st January 1815. Richard Webber of Horfield, Bristol, in a letter to the *Evening Post*, said that her tombstone bore the epitaph: 'Thou'll appear in greater power'. This tombstone was destroyed in an explosion in 1874 when a barge carrying gunpowder on the adjacent Regent's Canal blew up. It was, mysteriously, the only memorial in the whole cemetery to be shattered.

The sect that bore her name continued after her death and had many adherents in the district. In 1834 Ann Essam of Hampton established a Southcottian place of worship, believed to have been located next to her house near the Jolly Gardener inn, Uxbridge Road. When she died in 1844, leaving her considerable estate in trust for the printing and publishing of Joanna's writings, her daughter contested the will on the grounds that such a trust would be illegal because it was for 'the propagation of doctrines in opposition and subversive to the Christian religion'. The disappointed heiress claimed that the writings were blasphemous and immoral.

The case was finally decided by the Master of the Rolls in 1862. He concluded that Joanna Southcott had been a sincere Christian and that her works, though confused and incoherent, were written with a view to extend the influence of Christianity. However, he ruled that the will did come within the jurisdiction of the Statute of Mortmain, an ancient law forbidding the transfer of land ownership to religious corporations.

Meanwhile, a Yorkshire family had been appointed guardians of the oak box allegedly containing her sealed prophesies. Nailed shut, bolted and roped, it was said to hold not only her writings but also certain magical items that would end for ever all the troubles of the world – 'the Leaves of the Tree of Life for the Healing of the Nations'. Joanna's instructions stated that it could only be opened again in the presence of 24 bishops of the Church of England. If opened by anyone else, she said, its mystic powers would disappear.

In 1927 a famous psychic investigator, Harry Price, claimed to have opened it and discovered that it contained books, a pistol, a night-cap, a dice-box and a lottery ticket – but the Southcottians say that he opened the wrong box. A claim by the British Museum in 1966 that they had had the box but somehow mislaid it in their vaults was also denied.

The successors of the Millenarians or Southcottians still exist today as the Panacea Society. Shrewd investments have reportedly made the few surviving members extremely wealthy, on paper at least. According to Gerry Brooke writing in the *Bristol Evening Post* in 2004, the members of the society, now numbering about 25, 'have recently become increasingly secretive and allow no one except believers to view the cot or box or even to enter their Bedford headquarters which, they say, is the site of the original Garden of Eden'. It seems that they are now preparing for Shiloh's return in the year 2014. In fact, Mr Brooke says, they believe he has already returned and is occupying the body of Prince William.

How strange that a sect espousing such eccentric beliefs once gave spiritual comfort to poor labourers and servants living in hovels around Teddington and Twickenham!

ORTON
AND HALLIWELL

---❁---

Joe Orton is considered by many critics to be one of the finest playwrights of the 20th century. His surreal and cynical take on life and his sexual frankness are not to everybody's taste, however, and the manner of his death epitomises the dark side of the 'Swinging Sixties'. His name will for ever be linked with that of his friend and lover, Kenneth Halliwell. They shared a flat in Noel Road, Islington and first came to wider public knowledge in what might be entitled 'The Disgraceful Affair of the Defaced Library Books'.

In May 1962 they appeared at Old Street Magistrates Court charged with stealing and wilfully damaging 72 books from Islington and Highgate libraries. It was alleged that Orton (29) and Halliwell (35) had removed 1,653 colour plates from illustrated art books and had caused an estimated £450 worth of damage.

Examples of their literary vandalism were shown in court. A critical study of the poetry of John Betjeman had its title page defaced by a scurrilous sketch of 'a pot-bellied old man tattoed from head to toe and clothed only in a skimpy swimsuit.' The contents page to the first volume of Emlyn Williams' collected plays had acquired titles, including 'Knickers Must Fall', 'Up the Front' and 'Up the Back'.

The blank, bright yellow front flaps of books published by Gollanz were particularly vulnerable to modification by Joe Orton. He used to carefully remove them from their protective wrapping of library film and type spoof synopses, or blurbs, onto them. 'My blurbs were mildly obscene,' Orton admitted at the trial. 'When I put the covers back over the jackets you couldn't tell that the blurbs were not printed.' Halliwell told the court: 'I saw Orton typing on the covers of the books. I read what he typed. I considered them a criticism of what the books contained.'

Orton and Halliwell would replace the doctored books in their correct places and then watch the reactions of prospective borrowers who picked them off the shelves. 'I watched as people read them,' said Orton. 'It was very funny, very interesting.' The court did not share his amusement. The pair were jailed for six months each.

All this was welcomed as good publicity by the pair of ambitious literary homosexuals. It did Orton no harm at all and, with plays like *What the Butler Saw*, his star was in the ascendant. His original use of traditional elements of farce – sex and greed – to make darker, more profound comments on the futility of life, impressed critics and the more adventurous theatre-goers.

But for Halliwell, his companion's success was not so welcome. It was obvious to him and to everyone else that his was a greatly inferior talent. He was still welcome as Orton's partner in the gay community but the cultural world of the mid-sixties was not yet ready for such liberal attitudes. It became clear to Halliwell that his lover was under social pressure to ditch him and publicly espouse a more conformist lifestyle. He became increasingly jealous and frustrated.

Suddenly, in August 1967, it all became too much. In a fit of rage Kenneth Halliwell battered Orton to death and then stabbed himself. What would otherwise have been a sad and squalid little domestic tragedy became, because of the fame and talent of Orton, the focus of great public interest, its details of possessive homosexual passion being eagerly picked over by the prurient.

Orton's plays are still widely performed and are studied as set texts by students of English literature, those defaced library books from Islington and Highgate carefully preserved as relics of a revered genius.

THE HACKNEY HORROR

At first nobody really believed the four lads who came rushing back from the snow-covered Hackney Marshes on the evening of Sunday, 27th December 1981 claiming that they had encountered 'a giant great hairy thing' that reared up on its hind legs. 'We heard it growling,' said 13-year-old Tommy Murray. 'I shone my torch on it and saw it sideways in the dark. My dog Lassie did not want to go near it. I stood there for about ten seconds and then ran like hell.' They came across a middle-aged couple who said that they had seen it too and warned the lads to keep away in case it was dangerous.

Tommy was not the sort to tell tales. He had ambitions to be a zookeeper. He knew about wildlife and had no doubt that the tracks they had followed through the snow were those of a bear rather than just a big dog.

It was late in the evening but the boys' parents lost no time in reporting the matter to the police. The next day an extensive search of the marshes began. Fifty officers, some armed, together with dogs scoured the area. Some of the tracks the boys had seen were still there but the snow had by now melted somewhat and they were difficult to decipher. Others had been trampled on by the numbers of reporters, cameramen and sightseers who had converged on the area. They certainly could be bear prints, experts from London Zoo concluded, and it was definitely possible for a bear to survive there, despite Hackney Marshes being surrounded by houses and industry.

A shed on a nearby allotment was found to be damaged, as if an animal had tried to get in to find shelter during the cold night.

A set of prints were found at a sports centre and also claw-marks in the bark of a tree. Other children claimed to have seen the bear but it seems that they were just trying to get in on the action.

No bear was found and police began to suspect that they were the victims of a childish prank. A thaw had set in and a depressing drizzle removed the last traces of the so-called paw-prints. On the evening of the 29th, the *Sun* newspaper was contacted by a man who would only give his name as 'Ron', who claimed that the whole affair had been a hoax.

According to Ron, it had been thought out by a group of mates in a pub – 'just for a laugh'. They had got hold of a bear costume from a fancy dress shop and Ron himself had worn it out on the marshes to scare people that night. He said that it was him that the boys had seen and that other people had seen him getting out of a van. That seemed to be the end of the matter and the police were not best pleased with Ron – or the four boys. Strangely, the middle-aged couple who the boys said had also seen the bear never came forward to confirm the story, despite police appeals.

But somehow Ron's explanation did not fit the facts. The tracks in the snow had been identifed by the zoo's experts as being those of a bear. It would be impossible for a man in a fancy-dress bear suit to make such convincing prints, they said. Police were unable to find any theatrical costumiers who had hired out a bear suit around that time. The policemen who interviewed the boys were certain that they had not been telling lies. 'They were not hoaxers,' one officer commented afterwards, 'though they may themselves have been hoaxed.'

'The prints could not have been made by a hoaxer,' he went on, 'because no other prints were near them or led to them. But they could have been misinterpreted by all who saw them because by the time they were examined the snow had begun to melt and had then refrozen.' Afterwards someone made a cardboard model of a genuine bear-print and when this was put next to a photograph of the mystery print they were seen to be quite different. The real one was bigger and not exactly the same shape.

Yet two dead bears had indeed been found in the area earlier that same month. On 5th December a weir-keeper saw what he thought were two bodies floating in the River Lea. The police had been called to what was assumed to be the result of a suicide pact or a gangland killing. What was pulled out of the murky waters turned out to be the remains of two fully-grown brown bears, expertly decapitated and skinned.

No one knew how they got there or where they came from. The finger of suspicion was pointed at a travelling circus that had recently been in the vicinity. Had the two bears proved surplus to requirements and been disposed of at dead of night? Surely trained performing bears would have been been too valuable just to kill for the fur trade? They could have been sold on to another circus company or a fairground. Perhaps a rogue taxidermist had dumped the inconvenient innards into the river – yet the paws (which he would have needed intact) were still on the corpses when found.

Had one or more other bears somehow survived this butchery and escaped to roam Hackney Marshes in the dead of winter? Were they what the four boys had seen? If so, what happened to them? Are their descendants still out there somewhere?

The Lea Navigation, looking towards Hackney Marshes, where the dead bears were pulled from the water.

JACK THE STRIPPER
AND THE NUDES
IN THE THAMES

————— ❁ —————

On 2nd February 1964 the naked body of 30-year-old Hannah Tailford was washed up near Hammersmith Bridge. Her stockings were around her ankles and her panties stuffed into her mouth. Her face was badly bruised.

Hannah was the first in a series of prostitutes murdered in West London by a man whom the press soon dubbed 'Jack the Stripper'. When detectives visited her flat in search of clues they found that it had been turned into a makeshift photographic studio. There was a suggestion that Hannah had been using the pictures secretly taken in her flat to blackmail her clients.

More murders followed and they became known as 'The Nudes in the Thames' killings. Two months later, Irene Lockwood's body was discovered at Duke's Meadow, Chiswick, and links were made with the killings of two other prostitutes, Elizabeth Figg and Gwynneth Reed in June and November the previous year. On 24th April Helene Barthelemy's corpse was found near Swyncombe Avenue in Brentford.

Next, on 14th May, Mary Fleming, a mother of two, was found dead near a garage in Berymede Road off Acton Lane in Chiswick. Witnesses reported seeing a small van being driven out of Berymede Road at dangerous speed but no one had managed to get its number or a clear description of the driver. However, the traces of paint found on Mary's body and some of the others seemed to be a possible clue. They could indicate that the bodies had been held in or near a car-spraying workshop. It seemed likely that the killer was a van driver familiar with the local side streets at night.

Checks were made on individuals who fitted this description but no arrest had been made by November when another woman from the district was found dead in Horndon Street, off Kensington High Street. In his *Murder Guide to London* (1986), the writer Martin Fido suggests that the strong police presence in the Brentford, Chiswick and Acton areas had forced the killer to dump his latest victim well away from his usual territory. Police were convinced that they had narrowed the field down to three suspects and thought they had doubtless already interviewed their man.

This did not prevent yet another killing. On 15th February, Bridie O'Hara's body was found behind a shed at the Westpoint Trading Estate in Acton. This time Jack the Stripper had not had a chance to remove the body. The paint-spray workshop and

Mary Fleming's body was found near a garage on Berymede Road.

The River Thames at Duke's Meadow, Chiswick, where Irene Lockwood's body was found.

warehouse where the victims had been kept were located on the estate. When, soon afterwards, a South London man who worked on the estate as a security guard – one of the police's three suspects - committed suicide, leaving a note ambiguously saying that the pressure was 'all too much' for him, it seemed that the case had been solved. Police never named him but investigations into the Nudes in the Thames murders were brought to an end.

However, stories went around that things were not as simple as had first seemed. Rumours spread that Freddie Mills, the ex-light heavyweight boxing champion – who had been found shot dead in a car in Soho – was the real killer but this was firmly denied by the police.

Brian McConnell, an investigative journalist, came up with a startling theory in his book *Found Naked and Dead*. His suggestion was that the killer was in fact an ex-policeman who had had a long obsession with prostitutes and that the South

London suicide gave the police a convenient excuse to avoid the embarrassing revelations that the revealing of the true perpetrator would cause.

After the suspect's suicide, though, there were no more attacks so perhaps these ideas can be discounted. Jack the Stripper, whoever he was, brought feelings of fear and panic among local people, an atmosphere that was repeated in 2003 and 2004 after a series of attacks, some fatal, on young blonde women – decidedly not prostitutes – in the vicinity of Hampton and Twickenham. At the time of writing no one has been charged or brought to trial for these killings.

BONNIE & CLYDE AND THE CLEFT CHIN MURDER

---·❀·---

In the autumn of 1944, Elizabeth Jones was an 18-year-old ex-waitress and would-be striptease dancer living in Hammersmith, yearning for the drama and excitement that she felt was lacking in grey, bomb-scarred, food-rationed London.

Even as a stripper her curriculum vitae was not impressive. Her one performance in that line was, apparently, deemed 'unsuccessful'. She was desperate to do something really wicked and dangerous. Her dreams seemed to have come true when she met American army deserter Karl Hulten in a café. He described himself to her, inaccurately, as 'a big-time Chicago gangster'. Their fantasies intertwined and, losing touch with reality, they soon saw themselves as Bonnie and Clyde-style gangster and moll.

That night they went out for a ride in a stolen army truck. They met a girl cycling along the road and, to show Elizabeth Jones how tough he was, Hulten drove into her and robbed her of the few shillings that she was carrying. In the days that followed they terrorised West London, attacking and robbing cyclists and pedestrians. They offered another unsuspecting girl a lift, then knocked her out, taking her coat and handbag and throwing her into the Thames.

On 7th October they hailed a taxi driven by the unfortunate George Heath. The poor man just did not know what he was picking up. Hulten shot and killed him for the small amount of money he was carrying and later spent the cash at a dog track.

Heath's body was dumped at Knowle Green, Staines, near where the Spelthorne Council Offices now stand. Heath's distinctive appearance gave rise to the name, 'The Cleft Chin Murder', by which the case became known to newspaper readers.

Jones and Hulten now parted. Perhaps she had had enough. In a spirit of insane bravado Hulten had kept Heath's car. Police were able to identify it by tyre-tracks found on a grass verge near the body. This was his undoing. He was arrested in Fulham Palace Road on 10th October. A loaded gun was found in his pocket.

The end was greeted with some relief by Jones who must have realised how far she had fallen into degradation. A sympathetic police officer remarked that she looked pale. 'If you had seen someone do what I have seen,' she replied, 'you wouldn't be able to sleep at night.'

The trial was dramatic – each blamed the other for what had happened – but its outcome a foregone conclusion. Hulten was sentenced to death and Jones to imprisonment. Despite an appeal for clemency from the American Ambassador, Karl Hulten was hanged in 1945. Many felt that Elizabeth Jones should have met the same fate. 'She Should Hang' was chalked on walls beside pictures of a figure dangling from the gallows. However, it was recognised by the authorities that she had fallen under the spell of a charismatic but evil older man. She was imprisoned but quietly allowed to leave prison in 1954. Recalling the cases of Myra Hindley and Maxine Carr in more recent times, one wonders whether public opinion would let such a release happen today, even ten years after the event.

Writing about the case in 1946 in the magazine *Tribune*, George Orwell commented: 'it was almost by chance that they committed that particular murder and it was only by good luck that they did not commit several others. They were only together for six days and it seems doubtful whether, until they were arrested, they even learned one another's true names. The background was the anonymous life of the dance halls, movie-palaces, cheap perfume and the false values of the American film'.

THE LAST WOMEN
TO HANG

It is a grim coincidence that the last two women to be hanged for murder in Britain both met their deaths as a result of crimes committed in South Hill Park, Hampstead. The name of one has been almost totally forgotten but the execution of the other was a cause célèbre that hastened the eventual abolition of the death penalty.

In 1954, 11 South Hill Park was, like many of the properties in the road, divided into flats. On the ground floor lived Stavros Christofi, a Cypriot waiter, his German wife Hella and their two children.

It was Stavros's mother who was the cause of all the trouble. A jealous, passionate woman she had quite a history. At the age of 25, she had been tried but acquitted of the charge of trying to murder her mother-in-law by forcing a flaming torch down her throat! Recently come to England, she found fault with everything: the weather, the English language and especially how Hella was bringing up the children. Eventually the young mother could stand it no longer. Things had been fine before mother-in-law arrived. She decided to take the children on holiday to Germany and insisted that old Mrs Christofi must be back in Cyprus before she would return home.

Mother-in-law was not having that. She brutally attacked Hella using the ashplate from the kitchen stove as a weapon, knocking her out before strangling her as she lay on the kitchen floor, dragging the body out into the garden and setting it alight. A neighbour witnessing this assumed that she was setting fire to a tailor's dummy!

THE LAST WOMEN TO HANG

She then ran out into the street calling for help and saying that the kitchen was on fire and her grandchildren in peril. It soon became clear that she was lying in an attempt to cover up her own crime. She never accepted any responsibility for her evil deed, complaining to the last that Stavros had not bothered even to visit her in prison.

There was little public sympathy for Mrs Christofi but there was plenty for Ruth Ellis, who has the melancholy distinction of being the very last woman to be hanged for murder. She was perhaps her own worst enemy, a woman whose unfortunate choice of men friends and foolhardy honesty did for her in the end.

It might all have been different if the American airman who fathered her child when she was just 17 had not been killed shortly before the baby was born in 1944. Her marriage in 1950 to a dentist, George Ellis, lasted less than a year but now she was left with two children and no obvious way of earning a living.

She was not the first girl in her situation to be drawn into the world of seedy nightclubs and the earning of extra money by being specially accommodating to favoured customers. Yet she was honest and reliable and found a job as manageress of a club in Knightsbridge which paid quite well and provided her with a flat above the premises at 37 Brompton Road.

True the customers were a pretty mixed bunch but she was befriended by Desmond Curren, an older and quite respectable, unmarried businessman. She might have been fairly safe with him but she also caught the eye of a raffish racing driver with a liking for drink, David Blakeley. It was her unsuccessful juggling of these two relationships that led to her downfall.

Blakeley was the more charismatic figure. He soon charmed Ruth Ellis into bed and she had high expectations that he would marry her. But she was regarded by his family and friends as very lower-class and they made it clear that they despised her. Moreover, he was engaged to a young woman who was more socially acceptable to them.

Ruth Ellis lost her job at the club because of the antics of Blakeley and his drunken friends. The dependable Curren let her stay at his flat in Devonshire Street where Blakeley slept with her in Curren's bed. Eventually moving into a flat of her own, Ruth

The Madgala Tavern in Hampstead was one of David Blakeley's regular haunts.

remained in Blakeley's thrall but he still treated her just as a fluffy plaything.

In the spring of 1955 Blakeley dumped her and went to stay with friends at 29 Tanza Road off Parliament Hill, Hampstead. He refused to answer her phone calls and she began to suspect that he had another woman. Ruth called at his flat. There was no answer to her knock but she was convinced that she heard a woman's laughter from inside. She persuaded the compliant Desmond Curren to drive her up to Hampstead to see what was going on. She was not at all mollified to see Blakeley leaving the house in Tanza Road in the company of his friends' attractive young nanny. 'I had a peculiar idea then that I wanted to kill him,' she later admitted.

A week later, on the evening of 10th April, she took a taxi to Hampstead and went to one of Blakeley's regular haunts, the Magdala Tavern at the bottom of South Hill Park. Blakeley's car was parked outside. When he came out she shot him.

He staggered into the road and as he lay on the ground she fired at him three more times and then immediately gave herself up to an off-duty policeman who happened to be drinking in the pub at the time.

Ruth Ellis seemed fatalistically determined to suffer the ultimate consequences of her actions. She had killed Blakeley without any attempt at concealment and offered no defence. Her counsel had great difficulty in getting her to plead 'not guilty' for she regarded that as a lie. 'When you fired that revolver what did you intend to do?' she was asked in court. Her reply was scrupulously honest: 'It was obvious that when I shot him I intended to kill him,' she said calmly.

Despite the mitigating circumstances of how Blakeley had treated her, the death sentence was duly passed. Ellis wrote to Blakeley's mother accepting her punishment and expressing the hope that Mrs Blakeley would somehow understand her actions. In the days that followed, opponents of capital punishment collected some 50,000 signatures on a petition pleading for clemency but Ellis herself offered no support for their appeal.

She was hanged at Holloway Prison on 13th July 1955. Her death led to impassioned protests and was one of several contentious cases in the 1950s that soon afterwards brought about the end of capital punishment.

Long after Ruth Ellis was executed, her supporters continued their campaign on her behalf. In 2003 her appeal finally came to court before the Lord Justice of Appeal, Sir John Kay. He had some sympathy for their views, describing himself as 'astonished' that the original trial had lasted just one day. However, he pointed out that as the law stood in 1955 the trial judge 'was right to withdraw the defence of provocation from the jury' and that therefore the appeal must fail. Ellis, he said, 'had consciously and deliberately chosen not to appeal at the time' and, in contrast to the notorious case of James Hanratty and the A6 murders, no one disputed that she had killed Blakeley.

Sir John was publicly critical of the whole concept of posthumous appeals, regarding them as wasting valuable court time: 'If we had not been obliged to consider her case, we would perhaps in the time available have dealt with eight to twelve other cases, the majority of which would have involved people who were said to be wrongly in custody.'

He went on: 'Parliament may wish to consider whether going back many years into history to re-examine a case of this kind is a use that ought to be made of the limited resources available.'

In the summer of 2005 *Ruth Ellis: My Sister's Secret Life* was published by Muriel Jakubait. In this book, Mrs Jakubait claims that her sister was an unwitting victim of the Cold War between the West and the Soviet Union.

One of Ellis's society acquaintances was osteopath, Stephen Ward, later to be a key player in the Profumo Affair. They had, the book reveals, been close friends with links that went back many years.

Muriel Jakubait and her co-writer, Monica Weller, claim that Ellis and Blakeley were linked to the Burgess and Maclean spy scandal of 1951 and that Ruth was 'set up' by the authorities 'in a clever ploy to kill two birds with one stone'.

'They were in the thick of it,' Ellis's 84-year-old sister asserts. 'They knew too much.'

TUNNELS UNDER TOTTENHAM

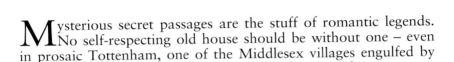

Mysterious secret passages are the stuff of romantic legends. No self-respecting old house should be without one – even in prosaic Tottenham, one of the Middlesex villages engulfed by London's working-class suburban sprawl in the 19th century.

You would probably expect to find them at Bruce Castle, an allegedly haunted building still in its own park and which now houses the local museum, and indeed there is a tunnel stretching – it is said – south-eastwards below Bruce Grove to Holy Cross Road. Another, apparently, leads three-quarters of a mile from the house to Downhills Park, coming up near an old water tower.

Black House, an old building that stood opposite the famous White Hart Lane, was at one end of a tunnel alleged to stretch for half a mile under the Tottenham High Road and Lordship Lane. Tottenham historian Fred Fisk, writing in 1923, said that he was told by the owner of a more recent house that by then stood on the site, that workmen attending to the drains came across a brick passage running southwards from a wall in the cellar. 'This passage looked too uninviting and the smell was too obnoxious' to persuade the owner to venture into it himself but apparently his son did explore it for some distance before the atmosphere became unbearable.

'As Henry VIII was a frequent visitor to Black House,' wrote Mr Fisk, 'there is no telling that he did not make use of this passage if occasion required or in one of his frolicsome moods.'

Locals at nearby Edmonton told tales that a man could walk half a mile from the former Weir Hall in Silver Street without seeing daylight. It was said that this tunnel was only used after a

All Saints church, Edmonton, where a secret tunnel was discovered in 1799.

death had occurred at the house, the body being spirited away for secret burial. It was deemed significant that the tunnel reached the surface in Bury Street – but the legends, almost forgotten these days, give no explanation as to why such secrecy should be deemed necessary.

In 1799 workmen apparently uncovered a tunnel leading away from Edmonton church, Fisk noted from the *Gentleman's Magazine* for that year. The subterranean passage was discovered after a large elm tree in the garden had been felled. It was in the form of a Gothic arch, three feet wide and four foot six inches high. The marks of the workers' tools could still be seen.

'Conjecture is,' said the magazine, 'that it was dug by Mr Muffet, vicar of Edmonton, from which he was ejected in 1642, being a powerful Royalist, either to secret himself from the Cromwellians, or to escape into the woods, which as tradition says, all the great common fields were, from Turkey Street to Long Hedge, Tottenham.' Escape he most certainly did, and survived to be reinstated to the living in 1660 on the restoration of Charles II.

It is not only the ancient historic buildings of the district that have stories of secret tunnels. The modern Broadwater Farm Estate became notorious in 1985 when Police Constable Blakelock was brutally murdered during the infamous Tottenham Riots. According to Charles Whynne-Hammond, to whose article 'Mysteries Under Our Feet' published in the *Weekly Herald* in 1976 I am indebted for many of these details, building work on the estate in the 1960s had to be suspended for several weeks when the ground was found to be unstable. It seems that laying the foundations of the blocks was made difficult by the remains of old passages, possibly old water courses and drainage channels.

If the ground suddenly swallows up an unfortunate footballer playing for Tottenham Hotspur at White Hart Lane, you will know what to blame!

MR SLUDGE,
THE MEDIUM

Spiritualism still has its advocates but most people now exhibit a healthy scepticism towards its more bizarre claims. In Victorian times it became quite a cult, despite the prevalence of organised religion, and its leading practitioners were international celebrities. One such was Mr Daniel Dunglas Home, of Connecticut, USA, who claimed in 1855 that he had 'received word from the spirits' that he should go to England for the sake of his health. He stayed in Ealing with a wealthy solicitor, Mr John Rymer, an ardent devotee of seances and the like. Rymer believed that Home had put him in touch with his son Wat who had died three years before.

Ealing did not have the social cachet of such places as Kensington or Chelsea and to have the great man staying in his house was quite a coup for Mr Rymer. He was anxious that his friends should have the chance to see what he could do.

Among these friends were Robert Browning and his wife, Elizabeth, who were invited to Ealing to meet Home. What happened that evening convinced Mrs Browning of the truth of spiritualism but persuaded Robert to write a lengthy and scathing poem lampooning all Home and his ilk stood for. He was immediately revolted by the obsequious way Home spoke to their fellow guests and his referring to the Rymers as 'mama and papa'. Moreover, he found him effeminate in the extreme.

Fourteen of them sat round a large table as the lights were dimmed, leaving just an oil lamp in the centre. Looking at Robert, Home cautioned them to behave themselves and to take seriously what was going to happen. The table began to vibrate and sounds of knocking on the table were interpreted by Home as the Rymers' son wishing to communicate with his parents. Home then asked some of those round the table to leave as he felt they were disturbing the spirits.

Those who remained experienced further strange manifestations. Elizabeth's dress was lifted as if by something under the table. Robert looked round but all hands appeared to be still joined. In the twilight something clothed in flowing muslin appeared opposite Elizabeth, rising and falling but never leaving the edge of the table. In a particularly strange happening, Home then announced that the spirit was going to play a tune on an accordian, held the instrument under the table and several tunes were heard by the bemused sitters! A clematis wreath passed from head to head in the manner of 'pass the parcel'. It ended its journey with Elizabeth who then passed it manually to her sceptical husband, as if to make a point. After more messages from young Wat Rymer, proceedings came to an end.

Elizabeth Browning was convinced that she had been in the company of a miracle worker. In a letter to her sister, she described seeing spirit hands that were 'very beautiful'. Robert, on the other hand, dismissed the whole charade as 'clumsy, below par even for a moderately good medium.' He said that the loose clothing that Home wore could conceal strings and other paraphernalia by which the effects could have been engineered. The discussions later that night in the Browning household in Wimpole Street must have been interesting to overhear.

The result of Robert's indignation was a 2,000 line tirade entitled *Mr Sludge, the Medium*, in which the whole business was dismissed as fraudulent. Dismissing Home as 'Dungball', a parody of his middle name, Browning elsewhere referred to him as 'a toady, a fraud, a leech, a braggart and a sot'. Elizabeth soon learned never to mention the subject of spiritualism in his hearing and warned her sisters to avoid it in their letters. The magazine *Punch* took Robert's side in the public argument that followed, printing a cartoon that showed Elizabeth as a goose, receiving the clematis wreath from hands that were only too obviously mechanical.

Rosemary Guiley, who retold this strange tale in *The Guinness*

Encyclopaedia of Ghosts and Spirits (1992), says that at the time it was believed that Robert Browning was somehow insulted that he had not received the wreath by supernatural means but only when Elizabeth handed it to him. This seems an unlikely explanation for his robust dismissal of spiritualism in all its forms. More likely, she thinks, he was scandalised by Home's effeminacy and suspected homosexual leanings. Even though Home married twice, there were persistent rumours about affairs with young men – quite enough for Robert to regard the man as beyond the pale.

Daniel Dunglas Home was certainly a controversial figure. His acolytes claimed that his paranormal powers revealed themselves at a very young age. It was said that his cradle rocked without assistance and that, at four years old, he correctly predicted the death of a cousin. As a medium he was often suspected of trickery but nothing was ever proved. The stage illusionist Harry Houdini later claimed that all his effects could be replicated by skilled conjurors if given the same performance conditions. He made the telling point that Home never gave public demonstrations and only held seances in private houses where it would have been considered exceedingly impolite, if not downright rude, for his hosts to suggest that their guest was cheating!

No Honour
Among Thieves

---- ❁ ----

Seventy-nine-year-old widower Henry Smith had made his house into a fortress. A wealthy retired engineer, he was paranoid about being burgled. He got his gardener to place man-traps and alarms in the extensive shady grounds of his home, Muswell Lodge, Tetherdown (off Fortis Green). Inside there were trip-wires designed to set off warning shots if any intruder stumbled over them.

But, as Gordon Honeycombe described in *The Murders of the Black Museum* (1982), it did him no good at all. On the morning of 14th February 1896 the gardener, Charles Webber, discovered Mr Smith's nightshirt-clad body on the kitchen floor. He had died as a result of a frenzied attack of twelve or more blows to the head, police concluded, possibly from two assailants. He had been trussed up using strips of tablecloth and gagged; two penknives used to rip the cloth lay beside the body. Also on the kitchen floor was a small lantern.

There was evidence that a jemmy had been used in an attempt to break in through the windows of both the sitting room and the scullery before the intruders gained access through the kitchen window. They had made quite a noise and Mr Smith had evidently been woken up and unwisely come downstairs to confront them. Presumably, after he had been attacked, the safe in his bedroom had been opened and emptied of cash and valuables.

It emerged that two men had been seen acting suspiciously in the neighbourhood over the previous two days. Detectives also discovered that a recently-paroled ex-prisoner, Henry Fowler, described as 'a large brute of a man', had been absent from his usual haunts. It seemed possible that he might have been involved in the robbery at Muswell Lodge.

When detectives called at Fowler's home his young brother-in-law identified the lantern as his. A £10 note stolen from the safe was found. A warrant was issued for the arrest of the 31-year-old Fowler and his regular accomplice, fellow labourer Albert Milsom (33) of Southern Street, Kings Cross. They were apprehended on 12th April at an address in Bath. Fowler resisted arrest and was repeatedly hit on the head with a police revolver.

Both men admitted going to burgle the house but blamed each other for the killing. Milsom claimed to have been out in the garden when the old man was killed and tried to ingratiate himself with the police by revealing where in the garden of Muswell Lodge they had hidden their burgling tools. Fowler claimed Milsom had done the deed.

There was no honour among thieves, it seemed. While the jury was out considering its verdict, Fowler attacked Milsom in the dock, almost strangling him. Police officers and court officials waded in to the melee and a glass partition was smashed. 'The members of the bar present and the rest of the spectators rose in their places in order to obtain a better view, many of them standing on their seats,' *The Times* reported.

The pair were unsurprisingly found guilty and received the death penalty. They were hanged at Newgate Prison on 9th June 1896, along with a Whitechapel murderer named Seaman. This has the macabre distinction of being the last triple execution ever to take place at Newgate. There were not unreasonable fears that the men would struggle violently. Four warders were in attendance, as well as the hangman, James Billington, and his assistant, Warbrick, a clergyman and other officials. In the confined space Billington pulled the lever of the trap while Warbrick was still standing on its doors. As the unfortunate Warbrick heard the sound of the bolt beneath his feet being drawn back, he instinctively grabbed the legs of one of the prisoners, ending up dangling over the pit, clinging on to the now-lifeless body.

It was perhaps because of this unedifying event that

Billington's successor as chief hangman, Henry Pierrepoint, devised an improved scaffold, described as 'the finest in the whole country, being fitted to hang three persons side by side.' When Newgate Prison was demolished to make way for the new Central Criminal Court, the Old Bailey, this grim contraption was moved to Pentonville where it was first used on 30th September 1902.

THE ACCOUNTANT'S
FEMALE FIGURES

---❁---

Putting your house on the market can be a complicated enough business at the best of times, without being distracted by visions of beautiful young women. In October 2004, a 65-year-old accountant told local newspaper reporter Terry Pattinson how a teenage blonde and a brunette in her early twenties visited his bungalow in Watersplash Road in Shepperton when he was working there alone. Far from welcoming their attentions, as

Bungalows in Watersplash Road, Shepperton.

some men of his age might have done, he said that he found the experience 'petrifying'.

It seems that he first saw the girls through his living room window. They were sitting on his garden seat, apparently engaged in conversation. The blonde he described as fifteen or sixteen years old, dressed in white and very pretty. The second girl, as attractive as her companion, was wearing a dark frock patterned with flowers. When he opened the door to confront them they disappeared.

'That was bad enough,' he said, 'but the next morning I went into the living room and saw the younger girl sitting on my couch. She was wearing the same white dress. I said, "For God's sake, leave me alone. Have I ever done you any harm?"'

'No,' the girl replied in a whisper – and then vanished.

Just then he heard a sound in the kitchen and saw the other girl standing there. After a few seconds she too disappeared. Later, while working upstairs, he heard the television come on and a song being played on his CD player. Coming down, he found both switched off. 'I recalled the song from the 1950s,' he told Mr Pattinson, 'but do not have it in my collection.'

'My wife thinks I'm nuts,' he admitted. 'This has never happened to me before. I am not a psychic. I am not a spiritualist and I have never believed in the world of spirits. My wife is the churchgoer in our family.' Nevertheless, he called in the local vicar who visited the bungalow and said a prayer. Since then the mysterious girls have not been seen there again, to his evident relief.

At the time of these visitations the accountant was in the process of selling the bungalow and moving to Sussex to be near his daughter and grandchildren. Would the possible appearances of such beautiful ethereal visions (as these girls seem to have been) be likely to reduce the value of the property or increase it?

A priest was also involved in a curious situation at nearby Ashford. Philip and Isobel Meyer had moved into Ashford Lodge, at the corner of School Road and Feltham Hill Road, in 1997. They soon became convinced that the house was haunted and called in the clergyman to bless every room in the place in an attempt to calm the restless spirit that was troubling them.

'For a few years things improved,' Isobel told local reporter Nathalie Herron in March 2004, 'but gradually the problems returned. One morning I was sleeping downstairs next to our new baby Jacob, who was in his carry-cot, when I was woken up by the feeling of cold air on my face. Yet the room had been warm and it did not feel like a draught.'

On one occasion Isobel had seen a light grey mist in the hallway and both Philip and Isobel had heard footsteps upstairs when they were alone in the house. A family friend, waiting outside the house in his car, saw Isobel walk past the window, followed by a shadow which he took to be her husband – yet Philip had been in bed upstairs at the time!

Six years before, when her elder son Louis was five, he went through a stage of not being able to get to sleep because, as he said, 'the voices would not let me'. Then there was the morning when his mother was helping him get ready for school and they heard a loud knocking on the wall. When they looked outside there was nobody there.

'We don't feel frightened,' Mr Meyer told Nathalie, 'but we would really like to know the history of the house and who lived here.'

Ashford Lodge in fact dates from about 1815. In Victorian times its owners were involved in a lengthy legal dispute with the family at nearby Ashford Villa who wanted to change the name of the house to Ashford Lodge. It ended up in the High Court in 1878 – but this hardly seems a likely explanation for the ghostly disturbances more than a century later.

Publication of the Meyers' strange experiences in the *Staines and Ashford News* prompted a letter from Mark Griffith who had lived next door at Flat 1, Ash Tree Court. 'It started one evening when we came home from work,' he wrote. 'I was preparing the dinner when I noticed a picture of a butterfly drawn on the kitchen counter. It looked like it had been drawn by a child and had just appeared while we were out at work.

'Later that night, while we were both asleep, I was woken by the sound of running water in the bathroom. I went to investigate and found the tap running. It was not just dripping, it was running fast like it had been turned on fully.

It took four or five turns to stop the water running. It really freaked us out.'

Was this a trivial case of simple forgetfulness at the end of a long day or the actions of a mischievous phantom? Who turned the tap on and who drew that strange little picture? Interestingly, the figure of a little girl was said to haunt a house in Tudor Road, also in Ashford, some years before. Could she have moved?

Whatever the truth in these particular cases, their publication in the local paper shows that there are still mysteries to be solved – even in the most prosaic and unromantic suburban districts of the former county of Middlesex.

Acknowledgements

Research for this book took me to libraries all over the county. The list of all the books and web-sites that I consulted is far too long to print in full. I have tried to acknowledge the sources used for the individual stories. For the historical background Michael Robbins' 1953 survey *Middlesex* (recently reissued by Phillimores) is still the best. Walter Jerrold's *Highways and Byways of Middlesex* (1909) has some good anecdotes and delightful illustrations by Hugh Thomson. The *Middlesex Quarterly* magazine, published in the 1950s, was another useful source. Also of interest is the series published by Phillimores and Historical Publications Ltd that includes Eileen Bowllt's *Ruislip Past* (1994) and Sheaf and Howe's *Hampton and Teddington Past* (1995) among many others.

There are a vast number of books and web-sites concerned with ghosts and the supernatural, many of which are in my bibliography for *Haunted Places of Middlesex*. They mostly have good indexes – which is important because stories from Middlesex are often very rare. Similarly there are shelves and shelves of books on 'real crimes' and murders. Perhaps the most useful for my purposes was Martin Fido's *Murder Guide to London* (Orion, 1986) which has several chapters dealing with crimes in the Middlesex suburbs.

I am particularly grateful to Barry Dix of the *Surrey Herald and News* (based at Chertsey but covering the Spelthorne area of Middlesex) for his help and also to Eddie Menday, local historian and columnist on the *Middlesex Chronicle*, who provided me with stories from the Hounslow area for this book, as well as for *Haunted Places* and *Lost Railways of Middlesex*.